HITOPADESA
OR,
THE BOOK OF GOOD COUNSEL

HITOPADESA
OR,
THE BOOK OF GOOD COUNSEL

TRANSLATED

FROM THE SANSKRIT TEXT

BY THE REVEREND

B. HALE-WORTHAM, B.A.

TRINITY COLLEGE, OXFORD
RECTOR OF DUNTON-WAYLETT, ESSEX
TRANSLATOR OF BHARTRIHARI'S "SATABAS," ETC. ETC.

GYAN

Published by

GYAN

Gyan Publishing House
5, Ansari Road
Daryaganj, New Delhi-110002
Phone: 011-47034999, 9811692060
E-mail: books@gyanbooks.com

Distribution Network
gyanbooks.com
India, USA, Canada, UK, Australia, France

ISBN : 978-81-212-2202-0 (HB)
First Published, 1906

2nd Impression 2021

Printed at: Gyan Press, Delhi.

Hitopadesa
or,
The Book of Good Counsel
Author: B. Hale-Wortham

HITOPADESA

OR,

THE BOOK OF GOOD COUNSEL

TRANSLATED

FROM THE SANSKRIT TEXT

BY THE REVEREND

B. HALE-WORTHAM, B.A.

TRINITY COLLEGE, OXFORD

RECTOR OF DUNTON-WAYLETT, ESSEX

TRANSLATOR OF BHARTRIHARI'S "SATABAS," ETC. ETC.

LONDON:

GEORGE ROUTLEDGE & SONS, LTD.

NEW YORK: E. P. DUTTON & CO.

TO

EVELINE,

COUNTESS OF PORTSMOUTH

IN MEMORY

OF

A LONG FRIENDSHIP

CONTENTS

PREFACE

"WITHOUT a parable spake He not unto them."

The parable, or the fable, which is only the same thing under another name, has always been the favourite Eastern method for conveying instruction. This of course immediately strikes the reader of the New Testament, where parables form so large a part of the Teacher's method and system. The same form meets us over and over again in the Old Testament, though perhaps it may not lie quite so much on the surface of the teaching. The parable or fable in Judges IX., under which Jotham conveys to his fellow-countrymen his belief in the mistake they had made in choosing Abimelech for their king—a person of low origin, the "bramble," from whom fire was to come forth and devour the "cedars of Lebanon," will immediately occur to the memory. Or again, the acted parable, when Ahijah met Jeroboam, and rent his new garment in twelve pieces, and said to Jeroboam, "Take thee ten pieces, for thus saith the Lord, I will rend the kingdom out of the hand of Solomon and will give it to thee" (I Kings XI. 30). Again, the book of Jonah, in the Old Testament, may perhaps be looked on in the light of a parable, the adventures which the prophet is said to have undergone being intended to teach certain spiritual truths. Apologue—fable

—story, with an underlying moral, comes natural to the Oriental mind. "Without a parable spake He not unto them." And so in a vast and miscellaneous literature, such as the classical literature of India, we should naturally expect to find instruction and wisdom conveyed under this form. The earliest collection of fables is that called the Panchatantra, or The Five Books, in which are collected some of the stories floating about the Eastern world at the time of its compilation. What the original text of the book may have been is difficult to say, in the face of the various alterations and expansions that it has undergone. Its existence in the sixth century A.D. is perfectly certain, when it was translated into Pahlavi by the order of King Nûshîrvân. Benfey, who has gone into the subject at some length, is of opinion that the original text rested on a basis of Buddhism, and that in course of time it underwent a number of important changes. He remarks also that, in consequence of these changes, a German translation made in the fifteenth century from a Latin rendering —the latter based upon an earlier Hebrew version —represents the original text more nearly than the existing Sanskrit form. A curious parallel to this is the hypothesis of Bentley, that, from Jerome's Vulgate, the fourth century text of the Gospels could be restored.

The *Panchatantra*, in one form or another, was known over the whole civilized world. An Arabic translation existed, made in the ninth century A.D., one in Hebrew, and one in Greek, from which versions it was translated into most of the languages of Europe, and was known in England under an English version entitled "Pilpay's Fables." We may say without exaggeration that we owe to India not only the idea whereby moral and spiritual truth is conveyed under concrete forms, but also some of those very identical forms under which this truth was originally conveyed to the Eastern peoples.

The *Hitopadesa*, or Book of Good Counsel, of which the following work is a translation, may be regarded as a recension of the *Panchatantra*. The *Hitopadesa*, however, underwent some considerable alterations, since it consists of only four books instead of five. This collection of stories first appeared in English in the translations of Dr. Charles Wilkins and Sir William Jones, made soon after the "discovery" of Sanskrit literature.

The translation which follows is for the benefit of those who do not know, and are not likely to have any acquaintance with, the original work, and it may therefore be as well to give some account of its plan and method. After an introduction, invoking the blessing of 'Siva, and extolling the excellence and the power of knowledge, and in which reference is made to the *Panchatantra* as one of the sources from which the book is derived, the fables begin in the following manner. A king called Sudarśana (the handsome) hears some one reciting a poem in praise of knowledge and wisdom. The poet shows how youth, riches, rank, and thoughtlessness, injurious as they are individually, are absolutely fatal in combination. The king's own sons, who possess all these drawbacks, not unnaturally occur to his mind, and he proceeds to meditate at some length on the unfortunate position of his family. His reflections lead him to call together an assembly of learned men and to ask their advice. He wants to know if there is any learned man in the kingdom who will instruct his sons. They are given to pleasure. They are vicious and ignorant; is there any one who will undertake to teach them the duties of their position and to regenerate them? A great Paṇḍit named Vishṇuśarman—a Brâhman, as his name implies, for the termination 'Sarman, which means shelter or refuge, is a common termination to the names of Brâhmans—politely remarks that princes sprung from great and noble families, such as that of which Sudarśana is the head, are quite capable of receiving instruction with advantage, and that he is prepared to take the king's son in hand. He compares the royal family to a mine of rubies, in which the common ordinary crystal is not to be found, and promises to teach the princes all that the king requires within the space of six months. Sudarśana, not to be outdone in politeness by Vishṇuśarman, rejoins, that "even an insect may attain to importance if it is in a flower on the head of the mighty," and that "even an outcast is enlightened by associating with the good." He gladly accepts Vishṇuśarman's offer, and hands over his frivolous, ill-instructed sons to their Brâhman tutor. Vishṇuśarman then seats himself on the terrace in front of the king's palace, and being wise enough to recognize the fact that his pupils are not likely to take the pill unless it is gilded, proceeds, after reciting a maxim of wisdom in verse, to relate for their amusement the fable of the Crow, the Tortoise, the Deer, and the Mouse, upon which maxim and fable the first book of the *Hitopadesa* is founded, setting forth the Forming of Friendship.

The fables then follow, but not in the manner which is familiar to us in Æsop, where each fable is a separate story, with its moral neatly appended. In the Indian work one fable leads into the other, and is interwoven with it, very much in the same way as the stories in the book which is familiar to us under the name of the Arabian Nights. The moral in fact comes first, and forms a sort of peg upon which to hang the fable. The clue of the fable with which each book begins is held in suspense until the end of the book, every intermediate fable having its own moral and its own conclusion. Interspersed throughout the fables are maxims of wisdom and morality, in verse. The fables themselves are in prose. The maxims are drawn from various treatises on law and morality—from the 'Satakas of Bhartrihari, from Chânakya, from Manu, and of course from the *Panchatantra*. These stanzas have, in fact, a distinctly Biblical ring, and many of them are very similar in expression to the maxims which meet us in the Hebrew Scriptures—in the Proverbs of Solomon, in Wisdom, and in Ecclesiasticus.

The *Hitopadesa*, as has been already said, consists of four books. Their titles are: 1, Mitralâbha, the acquisition of friends, or the forming of friendship ; 2, Suhridbheda, the separation of friends, or the dissolution of friendship ; 3, Vigraha, the way to make War ; and 4, Sandhi, the way to make Peace. Each book gives instructions on the subjects specified, and the moral is pointed by all kinds of characters — men, women, and animals — whose words and actions are intended to illustrate the right way of doing things by example, or the wrong way, by warning. The art of making friends, and the value of friendship when made, is illustrated by the way in which the Crow, the Tortoise, the Deer, and the Mouse assist each other, and the advantage to be gained from a friendship of this kind is shown by the escape of the Tortoise from destruction, helped by his three friends, who all live together ever afterwards in peace and happiness.

Separation of friends shows, under the disputes and misunderstandings which arose between a Lion and a Bull, who had been friends, how friendship can be destroyed by evil and backbiting tongues. "War" is illustrated by the battle between the Geese and the Peacocks, in which both armies suffer great loss, after prodigies of valour have been performed on both sides. Peace shows the way in which the damage was repaired by the skill of the ministers who were appointed to settle the differences between the contending powers. The intermediate stories in the book all go, more or less, to teach the doctrine set forth by the heading, and by the fable with which the book commences. The maxims which intervene, and carry on the argument, all have a suitable tendency.

The princes are represented as listening with respect and attention to their reverend tutor's exposition of wisdom and policy, but their enthusiasm is aroused by the subject treated of in the third book, relating to war. "Sir!" they say, "we are the sons of a Râja, therefore we desire to hear all about war." It is quite evident that the princes were not quite so ignorant as King Sudarśana had represented, for it must be understood that war was their special duty and calling. As Kshâtriyas—or warriors—their business was war. It was laid upon them by the obligations of their Varna or Caste and by a due performance of that obligation they might attain to blessedness. The Kshâtriya's duty was clearly shown in one of the most interesting of the sacred books of India, the *Bhagavadgîtâ*, or the Sacred Lay. In this poem, which is an episode in the great epic, the Mahabhârata, relating the fight between the two rival tribes, the Kurus and the Pândus, Arjuna, the hero and leader of the Pândus, is represented standing in his chariot, facing the host of the Kurus. He sees his fellow-countrymen drawn up before him; he hesitates; he doubts whether he ought to fight—to lead his forces on to the slaughter of their opponents. 'Siva puts on the form of his charioteer, and there, in the midst between the two armies, gives him a lesson on the duties of his calling, and tells him that perfection and righteousness is to be gained by following out the work laid upon him as a Kshâtriya, not by shirking it, and taking up some line of his own. A Kshâtriya, his divine charioteer tells him, may reach blessedness by the conscientious performance of his own duty, and in no other way; therefore he must fight. When the reverend Brâhman proceeds to discourse on war, the princes, as Kshâtriyas, feel themselves at home. They follow with eagerness the description of the acts of valour performed on both sides, and are so carried away by their feelings that at the end of the book they utter a maxim of wisdom on their own account, the only one attributed to them in the whole course of the instruction.

And so Vishṇuśarman sits on the terrace pouring forth with sententious gravity his maxims of wisdom, made endurable to his listeners by the fables with which they are interspersed, the princes regarding their superior, the learned Brâhman, with reverent attention, when Vishṇuśarman, at the end of the appointed course, turns to them and says, "Now, what more can I teach your highnesses?" the royal pupils answer, "Sir! through your kindness we have learnt the perfect round of our kingly duties: we are content"; and the lessons conclude with a benediction pronounced by Vishṇuśarman on the good and virtuous.

Such is the *Hitopadesa*—a book which comes to us across the centuries—a book of Eastern thought and Eastern wisdom. But in spite of the wide interval of time and place, there is much in it that is as true now as it was then, as true in the West as it was in the East: for it is a book of wisdom for all time, a book which speaks not to one nation, or to one period of the world's history, but to Humanity throughout all the Ages.

The following translation is intended for the general reader, and is an attempt to bring a "World Classic" into notice. The translation, therefore, as it is not meant for students or scholars, does not profess to be *literal*. The order of the Sanskrit original has been carefully followed, and so far the whole book has been faithfully translated. There are, as a rule, no condensations and no omissions. The only exception is, that twenty-two stanzas in the end of the fourth book have been omitted, relating to the different kinds of peace, which would be uninteresting and unintelligible to the reader. The work does not profess to encroach on the ground already occupied by the very excellent translation made by Professor Johnson, in 1848, for the use of the students of the East India College at Haileybury, and from whose Sanskrit text the following translation has been made.

I

INTRODUCTION

AND

MITRALÂBHA

ACQUISITION OF FRIENDS

HITOPADESA

INTRODUCTION

1 May the desires of the good be accomplished by the favour of Siva, whose crest is the new moon white as the foam of Ganges.

2 Those who listen to the *Hitopadeśa* gain skill in the use of Sanskrit words, as well as of a variety of phrases and the perfect knowledge of Political Science.

3 A wise man should think of knowledge and wealth as if death and old age did not exist. He should practise virtue as if death had seized him by the hair of his head.

4 Of all possessions wisdom is declared to be the best, for it cannot be taken away—it cannot be bought—it can never perish.

5 A river coming down from a high place makes its water mix with the ocean, so wisdom taking up its abode in the humble man makes him the associate of kings and partaker in great prosperity.

6 Wisdom gives discretion : from discretion a man gains office : from office comes wealth : from wealth, righteousness, and finally peace.

7 The science of arms, and learning gained from study, these two kinds of knowledge lead to

renown. The first becomes an object of ridicule in old age, the second is always held in honour.

8 As an impression made on a new vessel cannot be effaced, so under the guise of fables instruction is given to the young.

9 The way to gain friends: the severing of friendship: war: peace: these subjects are treated and drawn from the *Panchatantra* and other books.

END OF THE INTRODUCTION

There is a city called Pâtaliputra situated on the River Bhâgîrathî. Its ruler was a king called Sudarśana, endowed with all the virtues of a prince. One day he heard some one reciting the following verses:

10 Learning is the eye which clears up doubts and reveals hidden things. He who has not learning is blind.

11 Youth, abundance of riches, power, want of thought;—each of these by itself is a source of evil. How is it when they are all combined in one person?

When the King heard this, distressed at the ignorance of his own sons, who paid no heed to the Sacred Scriptures, and who were always engaged on wrong and frivolity, he thought within himself:

12 What advantage is there in the birth of a son who is neither wise nor righteous? What

profit is there in an eye that is blind? Is it not merely a pain?

13 A son unborn—dead—or a fool; it is better to choose the two first of these rather than the last. The first two cause grief once; the last continually.

14 He is born to some purpose by whom a family is raised to glory. In the world as it goes on who is not perpetually born again [after death]?

15 If a woman bear a son to him at whose name the chalk does not instantly fall at the enumeration of wise and virtuous men, what woman would be barren?

16 He whose mind is not given to liberality—devotion—heroism—the pursuit of wisdom—the gaining of wealth, he is only the excrement of his mother.

17 One wise son is better than a hundred foolish sons. One moon puts the darkness to flight, it is not dispersed by a hundred stars.

18 The son [which has been gained] by a very difficult penance, performed at a holy place of pilgrimage, should be obedient, prosperous, righteous, and wise.

19 Increase of wealth, freedom from disease, a loving wife, a wife with a civil tongue, an obedient son, and wisdom that is profitable to man—these are the six blessings in this world.

20 How should one be fortunate in possession of many sons [if they are but empty] measures

filling up the space in a granary? Only one is preferable if he be the support of the family and the glory of his father.

21 A father who accumulates debts is an enemy: a mother who does not walk chastely is an enemy: a beautiful wife is an enemy: a son devoid of understanding is an enemy.

22 Knowledge is poison in disuse: food is poison to indigestion: a king's court is poison to a poor man: a young wife poison to an old man.

23 A man who has a virtuous son is held in honour. A bow without a string—what use is it, though the wood be sound?

24 Alas, my son! Since you have passed your nights without study, in the midst of the learned you sink down, as one in the mire.

How then may these sons of mine be made wise and virtuous?

25 Eating—sleep—fear—offspring—on these points man is on a level with the animals. Virtue is his special characteristic. Without virtue man is even as an animal.

26 The man in whom neither virtue, wealth, passion, nor freedom from objects of sense are found;—his birth is as useless as the excrescences on a goat's neck.

27 Life, action, wealth, wisdom, and death;—
These things are man's destiny from his birth.

28 The destiny even of the mighty inevitably comes to pass. Nakedness is the destiny of Nîlakaṇṭha; sleep in the Serpent the destiny of Hari.

29 What has not been fated will never happen, nor can fate be avoided. This medicine is the antidote of care. Why not drink it?

But this is the maxim of idle persons careless of duty; for:

30 Even while thinking on destiny a man should not relax his efforts. There is abundance of oil in the Sesamum, but it cannot be extracted without labour.

31 Fortune waits on the Man of Spirit, the sluggard says "fate is everything". Contend with destiny—act with all your might. The fault is not yours if success follows not.

32 A chariot will not run on only one wheel: neither, without a man's own labour will fate bring things to perfection.

33 The [result of] deeds done in a former birth; that is what men call fate. Therefore act with vigour and be not weary in well doing.

34 As from a lump of clay the workman fashions what he will, so a man enters on the state fashioned by his own deeds [in a former life].

35 Treasure may fall in a man's way as the palm-tree fruit fell in the way of the Crow, but fate does not pick it up for him. It waits for him to make the effort himself.

36 Work is carried out by diligence, not by good intentions. The deer will not enter the lion's mouth when he is asleep.

37 The instruction of a father and mother makes a wise son; merely by being born he does not become learned.

38 The father and the mother who have left their son without instruction are his worst enemies. He cannot shine in the assembly of his equals any more than a heron among swans.

39 Though possessed of youth and beauty—though of noble family—men devoid of wisdom are at a disadvantage. They are even as the Kinśuka blossom that has no scent.

40 Even a fool is esteemed in the assembly if he wear fine clothes; a fool is thought some importance so long as he is silent.

Having reflected thus, the King called his wise men together. "Hear! my noble paṇḍits," he said. "My sons are always wandering from the right course, they are totally ignorant of the Sacred Scriptures. Is there any wise man among you who can put them in the right way and gain the new birth for them, by instruction in Political and Social Science?"

41 Glass from the proximity of gold gains the lustre of an emerald. Even so a fool if he be in the society of the wise may become clever.

42 The mind is demoralized by contact with the worthless. It becomes like those with whom it associates; so with the excellent it attains to excellence.

Then a great Paṇḍit named Vishṇuśarman, who was as accurately acquainted with Political and Moral Sciences as Vrihaspati himself, answered: "If the King be pleased, these your Majesty's four noble sons may learn the science you require from me.

43 Labour bestowed upon a thing of naught cannot profit. No amount of toil will make a heron talk like a parrot.

44 But this family is never wanting in sons of ability and virtue. How could crystals be found in a mine of rubies?

By six months' instruction I will make your Majesty's sons thoroughly conversant with Political and Social Science."

The King answered courteously:

45 "Even an insect, if it be on a flower, may ascend the head of the great; a stone if consecrated by a man of mighty power becomes divine.

46 Just as the Eastern mountain is lighted up by the nearness of the sun, so even the man devoid of excellence is lighted up by the nearness of the wise.

47 Good men know the difference between vice and virtue, but association with the bad may make them evil. A river rises with sweet water, but when it has reached the sea the water becomes undrinkable.

Therefore you shall be the instructor of my sons in Political and Social Science." So saying he handed over his sons with great respect to Vishṇuśarman. The Paṇḍit then by way of preface said to the Princes as they sat on the terrace on the front of the palace:

"Noble sirs! listen to me!

"Wise men spend their time in the study of Science and Poetry: fools in vice, sleep, and quarrels. Therefore to entertain your highnesses,

I will tell you the story of the Crow and the Tortoise, along with others."

The Princes answered "Sir! Tell us these stories." Vishṇuśarman replied, "Now attend! We will begin with 'The Forming of Friendship.' The first verse on this subject is as follows:

THE FORMING OF FRIENDSHIP

1 Men of friendly disposition, though destitute of means and wealth, speedily bring matters to a successful end like the Crow, the Tortoise, the Deer, and the Mouse."

"How was that?" said the Princes.

Vishṇuśarman said:

STORY I

On the banks of the Godâvari, there is a large Sâlmali tree, in which the birds, coming from various quarters, used to roost for the night. Once upon a time, when the night had come to an end, and the moon, the friend to the lotuses, was setting behind the Western Mountain, a Crow, named Laghupatanaka, happened to see a fowler approaching like a second Angel of Death, with his snares in his hand. On seeing him, the Crow thought to himself, "An unpleasant sight has occurred to me to-day the first thing in the morning; who knows what disagreeables are going to happen?" So saying, troubled in mind he followed the fowler: for:

2 As occasions of sorrow and of fear arise, the mind of the fool is troubled. But at things like

these the wise man is not disturbed. For people who have work to do in the world must certainly not allow themselves to be unduly harassed.

3 As we rise each morning danger is near us: we should reflect; what death—danger—sorrow may befall to-day?

Eventually the fowler spread his nets, scattered some grains of rice under them, and hid himself. Just at that moment Chitragrîva, the king of the pigeons, came flying along with his retinue. He saw the grains of rice, and said to his attendant pigeons, who were anxious to pick up the grains, "How is rice going to be produced in an out-of-the-way forest? This wants consideration. I cannot look on this as a piece of good luck. Perhaps our greediness after the rice may put us into the same position as

4 The traveller, who in his covetousness after a gold bracelet, fell into an impassable quagmire and was seized and eaten by a tiger."

"How was that?" asked the pigeons.

The king of the pigeons said:

STORY II

One day, when I was feeding in the Southern Forest, I saw an old Tiger, who had been bathing, and had some Kusa grass in his paw. He stood on the edge of the pond and kept calling out: "Hallo! Traveller! take this bracelet of gold." A traveller happened to be passing by and heard the voice. He was a covetous man, and he thought within himself that he had fallen on a piece of good luck. But he had doubts as to whether it would be prudent to accept a gift from such a source; for:

5 In an attempt to gain something from an inauspicious quarter, no good result can be looked for. Wherever poison is about, there even Amrit may be deadly.

But then there is always a certain amount of risk in the getting together of money. So it is said:

6 If a man does not overcome his doubts, nothing seems good to him; but if he get the better of his doubts and his life is prolonged, he will come across something worth having.

Well, then, I will look into the matter. He then said, "Where is this bracelet?" The Tiger stretched out his paw and displayed it. The Traveller said, "But how am I going to trust a savage creature like you?" The Tiger replied, "It is quite true! When I was young I was very dangerous. I killed a large number of cows, Brâhmans, and men. In consequence of this my wife and children died. Now I am solitary. Being in this state, a holy man, whom I met one day, advised me to practise the duty of liberality. I followed his advice. I am regular at my ablutions, I am generous and merciful. Besides this I am old, my teeth are gone, and I have lost my claws. Surely I am an object of confidence. For:

7 Sacrifice, study of the Sacred Scriptures, almsgiving and penance: Truth, fortitude, patience,

and freedom from covetousness : Tradition tells us that this is the eight-fold road leading to righteousness.

8 The first four may be practised out of ostentation, but the second four exist only in the single-minded.

I am so absolutely free from covetousness that I am willing to give anyone this bracelet of gold, which I have in my hand. Still, it is hard to persuade men that there is no truth in the idea that the Tiger is a devourer of men ; for:

9 The world following past ages holds up to us as religious examples—a procuress preaching morality, and a Brâhman who slays cows. Besides, I have studied religious books. Listen to what I say :

10 As rain on parched ground, so is a gift of food to a hungry man ; liberality displayed to a poor man brings forth much fruit, O son of Pâṇḍu.

11 Life is as dear to others as it is to oneself. Good men bear this in mind, and are merciful to all living creatures.

12 In giving and in refusing : in pleasure and in pain : in things agreeable and disagreeable : a man has a sure guide by considering his own feelings.

13 A wise man looks on another's wife as his own mother ; on the possessions of another as a clod of earth : on all creatures as himself.

You are poor and distressed, therefore I am anxious to give you something ; for it has been said :

14 Nourish the poor: make no presents to the rich: medicine is for the sick man; what have the healthy to do with medicine.

15 It is a duty to give. A gift to one to whom one owes nothing, at the right time and place—a gift to the proper object: that gift makes for righteousness.

Therefore bathe in this lake and accept the bracelet of gold."

The Traveller's misgivings were dispelled, and he proceeded to bathe in the lake. No sooner had he entered the water than he sunk in the mud and was unable to escape. The Tiger seeing him stuck fast, said "Be of good cheer, I will lift you out of the mud." So saying he slowly approached the Traveller. The Traveller being within the Tiger's clutches, thought to himself:

16 That he reads not the Sacred Scriptures, that he studies not the Vedas—this is not the reason of his evil doings. It is the innate qualities of the evil man which prevail in him, just as the milk of the cow is naturally sweet.

17 A devotional act (performed) by a person whose mind and senses are not in subjection is (as useless) as the washing of an elephant. Knowledge without devotion is as (out of place) as an ornament on a woman disliked by her husband.

I made a great mistake in placing any confidence in a savage animal: for it is said:

18 Confidence should not be placed in rivers: nor in those who carry weapons: nor in animals

which have horns or claws: nor in women of royal families.

19 The natural disposition of each person, not his acquired virtues, is tested by circumstances. For the natural disposition gets the mastery of all the other qualities, because it lies on the surface.

20 The moon in its passage through the sky dispels the darkness; with its thousand rays it goes through the hosts of stars. Yet in accordance with destiny it is swallowed by Râhû. Who then can escape the destiny written on his forehead?

While the Traveller was engaged in these reflections, the Tiger killed and ate him. Therefore I say: the Traveller, who in his covetousness after a gold bracelet, fell into an impassable quagmire was seized and eaten by a Tiger.

Nothing therefore ought to be done without careful deliberation; for:

21 Food that has been well digested: a clever son: a well-instructed woman: a king well served: a speech carefully considered: an action well deliberated; These things will never change for the worse, however much time may have passed.

One of the pigeons hearing this said with impatience, "What is this that I hear?

22 The advice of the old should be listened to when danger is impending: respect is always due to them.

But why need we ask permission to eat?

23 All meat and drink on the earth is beset with danger. How then is any business to be taken in hand, or how is life to be maintained?

24 The envious: the censorious: the dissatisfied: the wrathful; the suspicious: the man who lives dependant on another. These six classes are partakers of misery."

On hearing these words the pigeons alighted, for:

25 Even learned men—versed in the deepest science—able to resolve doubts—fall into misfortune when they are blinded by avarice.

26 Through avarice wrath gains the mastery: through avarice desire comes into being: through avarice is produced confusion and destruction. Avarice is the root of all evil.

27 The birth of a golden deer is impossible; yet Râma desired a deer of this kind. Often, when disaster is approaching, the mind of men become darkened.

The pigeons were then immediately caught in the net; and in consequence they all fell foul of him by whose evil advice they had been trapped; for as it is said:

28 One should not go in the front of one's tribe. If the result (of the expedition) is successful the reward is equal to all: if there be a failure the leaders are the first to fall.

29 Unbridled passions lead to destruction: victory over them is the road to prosperity. You may go by whichever you please.

Chitragrîva hearing the abuse showered on the unfortunate adviser said : " It is not his fault, for :

30 When calamities begin to fall even a friend may make them worse ; even as the leg of the cow is made the post to which the calf is tied (at milking time). Then further :

31 He is a true friend who is able to rescue one fallen into misfortune ; he is not a friend who is only clever at finding fault with the plans for recovery.

In a time of disaster it is the mark of a coward to lose one's head. Let us then be courageous and consider what is best to be done ; for :

32 In misfortune firmness : in prosperity moderation : in the assembly clearness of speech : in war bravery : for glory ambition : to the study of Holy Writ intense application : on these points the disposition of the noble-minded is perfect.

33 A man who displays calmness in prosperity : cheerfulness in adversity : steadfastness in battle : is rarely born into the world. Such a man is the joy of the whole earth.

34 Six evils must be overcome in this world by a man who desires prosperity : Sleep, sloth, fear, anger, idleness, procrastination.

Therefore I advise that we should all combine, take up the net and fly away with it ; for :

35 A matter can be carried out by a combination of even the very smallest things. A furious elephant is bound by blades of grass twisted into a rope.

36 Alliance with their own families, though they be but humble, is best for men. Grains of rice shaken out of their husks will not sprout."

The pigeons then, taking Chitragrîva's advice, took up the net and flew off. The fowler seeing this from a distance—thought to himself, as he ran after them:

37 This flock of birds together have carried off my net; but they will settle down again presently and then I shall catch them.

The pigeons, however, soon flew out of sight, and the fowler giving up the pursuit, returned to his place. The birds then addressed their leader and said: "Sir! what is to be done now?"

Chitragrîva answered:

38 "A father is a friend, and a mother is a friend: one more (besides these) may be a friend from his natural disposition. But others may become friends from what they expect to gain.

I have a friend called Hiranyaka, the king of the mice. He lives in a delightful wood on the banks of the Gandakî. I will get him to come and gnaw the net asunder with his sharp teeth and let us out." They went therefore to the hole which Hiranyaka had made. It had a hundred outlets, for he lived in continual apprehension of danger.

39 An old mouse learned in science and policy, able to foresee danger in the distance, lived in a hole with a hundred openings.

Hiranyaka was alarmed at the noise the pigeons

made in their descent, and remained quiet within his hole. Chitragrîva cried out: "Friend Hiranyaka, will you not give me a welcome?" Hiranyaka, recognizing Chitragrîva's voice, was delighted, and ran out saying, "My dear Chitragrîva, I am delighted to see you!"

40 There is no one happier in the world than the man who has a friend to talk with—a friend to live with—and the sympathies of a friend.

Then seeing the net, he said with astonishment: "But what is the meaning of all this?" Chitragrîva replied, "This is the result of our actions in a former birth; for:

41 Exactly in proportion as his deeds have been good or bad, so is reward or punishment measured out to man by the Creator.

42 Sickness, sorrow, pain, bonds, affliction: These are the fruits of the tree of man's transgression.

Hiranyaka, hearing this, ran forward hastily to sever the bonds which held Chitragrîva. But Chitragrîva said: "Not so," my dear friend; "first loose these followers of mine." Hiranyaka replied, "I am weak, and my teeth are brittle; am I to gnaw asunder the snares which hold your followers? If my teeth do not break, I will first let you out, and then I will do the best I can for the others." "So be it," replied Chitragrîva. "Still, I pray you, do your best to free them too." Hiranyaka answered: "To save one's dependants at the sacrifice of one's own life is not approved of by those skilled in the science of morality; for:

43 A man should guard his wealth against misfortune, by his wealth he should guard his wife, but he should always employ his wife and his wealth to guard himself.

44 The lives of men are the means for attaining righteousness, wealth, pleasure, and final emancipation; by destroying life, what is not destroyed? by preserving life, what is not preserved?"

"My dear friend," said Chitragrîva, "such may possibly be the rule of moral science, but I cannot bear to behold the misfortune of those who are dependant on me: Therefore I beg this of you; for:

45 An enlightened man will give up even riches and life for the sake of others: what can be better than renunciation of all things for the sake of the good, since death is certain?

There is, too, another argument that is unanswerable:

46 These my followers are my equals in birth, possessions, and virtue: Tell me, then, what fruit is my superiority in rank to gain for me?

47 They follow me closely, yet they gain nothing by it. Therefore save these my friends at the expense of my own life.

48 O my friend! think nothing of this perishable body of mine: preserve only my reputation.

49 If glory may be gained—glory everlasting and spotless—by (the sacrifice of) a body full of impurities, and which passes away—then why should I not gain this glory?

50 The difference between the body and the virtues is infinite; the body perishes in a moment, the virtues live for ever."

Hiranyaka, on hearing these noble sentiments, was filled with delight. He exclaimed: "You have spoken nobly! The sovereignty of the three worlds is the lawful portion of one so considerate to his dependants." He then gnawed the net asunder and the pigeons escaped. Hiranyaka, after solemnly congratulating the birds on their deliverance, turned to Chitragrîva and said, "This imprisonment in the net was in accordance with the decree of destiny: it is not reasonable that you should look on it as owing to your fault; for:

51 A bird which sees a piece of flesh a hundred yojanas distant, when his destined time is come does not see the snare (though it be close by).

52 When I beheld the eclipse of the sun and moon: When I see the binding of the elephant and the serpent: When I see the indigence of a wise man: I exclaim: 'Ah! how powerful is fate!'

53 Even birds who wander in the sky alone meet with misfortunes: Fish are caught by skilled fishermen even in the fathomless sea: Since fate is so froward, what matters well doing? What profit to a man is a firm abiding place? For death, stretching out his hand to inflict calamity, strikes even from a distance."

Hiranyaka, having uttered these wise sayings,

exercised the due rites of hospitality and dismissed the pigeons, who went on their way under the guidance of Chitragrîva.

54 Friends should be made of every kind and to any number. See how the pigeons were loosed from the snare by the friendship of a mouse.

After the pigeons had gone, Hiranyaka went back into his hole, when a Crow called Laghupatanaka, who had been a spectator of the whole proceeding, cried out with admiration: "Hiranyaka! your behaviour is most praiseworthy! I desire the honour of your acquaintance. I pray you let me form an alliance with you."

Hearing this, Hiranyaka, still keeping within his hole, answered, "And pray who may you be?" The Crow replied, "My name is Laghupatanaka. I am a Crow." Then said Hiranyaka, laughing, "How can there be any friendship between us? for:

55 In this world a wise man will always unite things together which have some affinity. I am the food, you are the eater: how can there be any friendship between us?

56 Friendship between the food and the eater must always be a source of misfortune. A deer that was trapped in a net by the cunning of a jackal was rescued by a crow."

"How was that?" inquired the Crow. Hiranyaka said:

STORY III

In Magadhadésa there is a forest called Champakavati, and in it lived a Deer and a Crow who were great friends. The Deer, who was well fed and fat, was roaming about and fell in with a Jackal. The Jackal on seeing him said to himself, "I should like to make a meal off this tender beast. I must try and worm myself into his confidence." So saying he approached the Deer and saluted him affectionately. "Who are you?" said the Deer. The Jackal replied: "I am Kshudrabuddhi the Jackal. I live in this forest all by myself; I have neither friend nor relation—indeed I am as good as dead; but now that I have found a friend in you, I seem to have come back to life again. I will be your humble servant." "I am delighted to make your acquaintance," answered the Deer. When evening came the two newly-made friends went to the Deer's abode. In the neighbourhood lived a Crow, called Subuddhi, an old friend of the Deer. Perched upon a Champaka tree he saw the Deer and the Jackal approaching, and called out to the Deer, "Who is your friend?" The Deer replied, "He is a Jackal who is very anxious to form an alliance with us." The Crow answered, "This sudden confidence in a new-comer is most improper. You have made a great mistake; for:

57 One whose family and disposition are unknown should not be taken in as a guest. The vulture Jaradgava was killed through the fault of the cat.

"How was that?" said the two friends. The Crow said:

STORY IV

On the banks of the Bhâgîrathî is a mountain called Gridhrakuta. Upon this mountain grows a large-leaved fig tree with a hollow trunk, in which lived an old Vulture called Jaradgava. He was almost blind and had lost his claws; the birds, therefore, who lived in the same tree, took compassion on him, and each contributed to his maintenance a trifle out of his own store. Upon this Jaradgava lived, and in return looked after the young birds when the parents were away. One day a Cat, whose name was Dîrghakarṇa came to the place with the view of preying on the young birds. On seeing the Cat approaching, the small birds set up a screaming overwhelmed with terror, and Jaradgava hearing the noise, called out, "Who is this coming here?" Dîrghakarṇa saw the Vulture, and being terrified said to himself, "O dear! I am done for! Still, however—

58 As long as danger is at a distance it is but an object of fear; but when it comes into the immediate neighbourhood, measures must be taken to meet it. So as I am too near to run away, fate must have its course. I will go and speak to the Vulture."

With this resolution he approached the Vulture and said, "Sir! I hope your honour is well." "Who are you?" rejoined the Vulture. The other replied, "I am a cat." Then take yourself off at once," said Jaradgava, "or I will be the death of you." The Cat replied, "Only hear what I have to say first, then after that, if you think that I am worthy of death, you may kill me. For:

59 Is there any place on this earth where a man is punished or rewarded simply on account of his birth? He is punished or rewarded according to his behaviour."

The Vulture said, "Well, what business do you follow?" The Cat replied, "I live here on the bank of the Ganges, I perform daily ablutions, I abstain from flesh, I practise the task Chândrâyana, as is the usage of religious students. The birds who are the object of your care and affection, are always extolling your knowledge and excellence; and therefore I have come here to learn the law from you who are advanced in years and wisdom. How is it that you look upon it as your duty to kill me who am your guest? For the duties of a householder have been declared as follows:

60 Hospitality, such as is usual, must be shown even to an enemy when he has once entered the house. A tree does not refuse its shade to the man who is cutting it down. But if there is no food to offer, a stranger ought at least to be greeted with civility; for it is said:

61 Straw, room, water, and civil language: These four things are never refused to any in the house of a good man.

62 Whosoever may arrive at the house—whether a child, or an old man, or a young man, he must receive due respect. The visitor is the superior of all.

63 Good men show compassion even to beings that are worthless. The moon does not refuse her light to the house of a Chânḍâla.

64 When a guest departs from the house with his wishes ungratified, he leaves the credit of his own evil deeds to the inhospitable householder, and takes away as his own such virtues as belong to his host.

65 Even a humble man of the lowest caste must be hospitably received. A guest is all the deities in his own person."

The Vulture replied: "It is well known that cats love flesh, and there are some young birds living here; hence my words to you." On hearing this the Cat bowed himself to the ground and said: "As for me, I have performed the Chândrâyana penance, I have studied the Sacred Scriptures—I have become free from passion and attachment. For the divine writings, however much they may differ on other points, all agree in teaching that it is a paramount duty to abstain from injury; for:

66 Men who refrain from injury to others: men who bear all things with patience: men who are a refuge for all creatures: these are on the road to heaven.

67 Righteousness is the only friend which follows men even after death; everything else goes to destruction with the body.

68 When one eats the flesh of another, consider the difference which there is between them. The gratification of one of them is momentary, the other loses his life.

69 Even an enemy would be spared by a man who really perceived the pain that is felt by one at the point of death.

70 Who would commit a crime for the sake of satisfying his hunger, when he could fill his belly with roots and fruits that grow of their own accord in the forest?"

By the utterance of these sentiments the Cat so far gained the Vulture's confidence, that he was allowed to remain in the hollow tree, and day after day catching the young birds he brought them into the hollow of the tree and ate them. The birds then, perceiving their young ones continually disappearing, were filled with lamentation, and proceeded to hold an inquiry. The Cat, on finding this out, slipped away and escaped. The result of the investigation held by the birds was, that they found the bones of their young in the hollow tree, and concluding that the Vulture was the culprit, they all set on him and killed him. Therefore I say that, one whose family and disposition are unknown should not be taken in as a guest.

When the Jackal heard this story he was angry, and said, "When the Deer first saw you, your disposition was unknown to him; how then do you account for his continually increasing friendship with you?

71 Where there are no wise men, a man of small intelligence is thought much of: in a country where there are no trees, the castor-oil plant is reckoned as a tree.

72 'Is this man one of us, or is he a stranger?' This is what narrow-minded men say. To those of liberal disposition the whole earth is but one family.

"This deer," continued the Jackal, "is my friend; therefore you are my friend too." "What is the good of all this disputing," exclaimed the Deer. "Let us all three live together in peace and harmony; for:

73 All men have both their friends and their enemies: The way in which a man is looked upon depends on his behaviour."

Finally the Crow gave way and said: "Well, so be it," and in the morning they all went to their favourite haunts. One day the Jackal said confidentially to the Deer, "I can tell you where there is a field full of corn: if you like I will show you the way." So the Deer went along with the Jackal, and finding the field, spent several days there, feeding to his heart's content. At last the owner of the field saw him, and set a trap. The next day, when the Deer came as usual to feed, he was caught in the trap. The Deer reflected, "How am I to escape from this trap, deadly as the snares of death, except with the help of a friend?" While these thoughts were passing through his mind, the Jackal came to the spot elated with the idea of his plan being successful, and expecting to make an ample meal on his friend the Deer. The Deer was overjoyed on seeing him, and cried out, "My dear friend! Break these bonds! Get me out without delay; for:

74 Misfortunes prove a friend: battle a brave man: a loan an honest man: lessening fortune a wife: affliction a relation.

75 The man who will stand by another in affliction as well as at a feast: in calamity, in a famine, in a tumult: who will follow him even to the King's Court or the Cemetery—he is indeed a friend."

The Jackal carefully examined the snare, and thought to himself: "Well! the Deer is caught fast enough." So he said, "My dear friend, this trap is made of sinews; now to-day is Sunday, and you cannot expect me to touch it with my teeth to-day: this will never do. But if you will wait till to-morrow, I will come and do whatever you may desire." Meanwhile the Crow, finding that the Deer had not come home in the evening, went to look for him, and finding him in the trap said: "What is the meaning of this?" The Deer replied, "This comes of not taking your advice. As it has been said:

76 Misfortunes follow close upon him who will not listen to the advice of his well-wishers. He becomes the laughing stock of his enemies."

"But where is the Jackal?" said the Crow. "There he stands," replied the Deer, "waiting to eat me up." "I told you as much," answered the Crow; "for:

77 Though a man may say, 'I have committed no crime,' this is no reason for confidence in him. There is always danger to good men from the evil.

78 The friend who praises another to his face and abuses him behind his back, should be avoided. He is a jar of poison with milk on the top."

The Crow heaved a deep sigh and exclaimed, "You deceitful wretch of a Jackal! See what you have done!"

79 It is easy enough to deceive confiding persons, who are taken in by honied words, and cheated by pretended services.

80 O earth, our mother! how canst thou endure the treacherous, who act with villainous deceit towards their benefactors, simple-minded, kindly men.

81 No acquaintance, no friendship should be made with the evil. Charcoal burns the hand when it is hot, blackens it when it is cold.

But this is the way of the treacherous man.

82 He flatters you to your face: he takes away your character behind your back. He is overflowing with compliments. But if he discovers any weak point in you, he attacks it without mercy. The treacherous man is like a gnat.

83 If an evil man speak kindly, have no confidence in him; with his tongue he distils honey, but in his heart is deadly poison.

Early the next morning the Crow saw the farmer who owned the field coming with his stick in his hand. He said to the Deer, "Lie down and pretend to be dead: when I give you the signal, jump up and run away." The Deer did as the Crow told him. The farmer came up, and seeing, as he supposed, that the Deer was dead, was delighted, and disentangling him from the snares of the trap, he began to gather them together. As soon as he had gone a little distance off, the Crow gave the signal, and the Deer jumped up and made off. The farmer turned round, and seeing the Deer running away, threw his stick at him in a rage, which missed the Deer and killed the Jackal; for as it has been said:

84 Even in this world, sooner or later, a man gains the reward of his vices or of his virtues.

Therefore I say: Friendship between the food and the eater must always be a source of misfortune.

The Crow replied:

85 "Even if I had eaten you, there would not have been enough to satisfy me: while you live, I shall live too, as harmless as Chitragrîva.

86 Confidence in others is only shown in those who have good dispositions themselves. The natural character of the virtuous man is never changed for the worse.

87 The mind of the good man undergoes no change, though it may be roused by anger. The water of the ocean cannot be heated by a straw fire."

Hiranyaka said: "But you are naturally fickle, and with a fickle man no friendships should be made; for it has been said:

88 A cat, a buffalo, a ram, a crow, a bad man: these gain the ascendancy only when men

are led to trust them. Therefore confidence should not be placed on any of them.

89 With an enemy an alliance should not be made, however clear may be the treaty. Water, though it be warm, will quench the fire.

90 A bad man should be avoided, though he be adorned with learning. A serpent wears a jewel as an ornament, but he is none the less dangerous.

91 What is impossible cannot be done, what is possible may be done. A cart will not float on the water, nor will a boat travel along a road.

92 He who relying on his wealth puts his trust in an enemy, or in a disloyal wife, is the author of his own downfall."

Laghupatanaka replied: "I have heard everything; but for all that I am perfectly determined that you and I must be friends; otherwise I will starve myself to death at your door; for:

93 A bad man is like a clay pot—easy to break, difficult to mend. A good man is like a gold pot—difficult to break, easy to mend.

94 Metals combine because they can be fused together: birds and animals combine through instinct: covetousness and danger join fools together; virtue is the bond of union between the good.

95 Good men are like the cocoanut: bad men like the fruit of the jujube: only good to look at.

If you understand this, you will desire the companionship of the good, for:

96 Even with the cessation of friendship, the feelings of the good change not. Though the lotus stalk be broken, the fibres still remain intact.

97 Single-minded—liberal—constant—the same whether in prosperity or adversity—kind—straightforward: A man who is all this is a true friend.

Where am I to find any one endowed with all these qualities except you?" When Hiranyaka had heard all this, and a good deal more of the same kind, he came out of his hole and said: "Such excellent maxims as you have uttered are indeed refreshing; for it has been said:

98 A bath of the coldest water—a necklace of pearls—ointment of sandal—these things are refreshing to one overcome by the heat; but the conversation of virtuous men, adorned with attractive charm and sound reasoning, is still more refreshing to the mind.

99 Betrayal of secrets, importunity, roughness, instability of mind, wrath, want of truth, gambling: these are the destruction of friendship.

100 Ability and Honesty in a man can only be known by dealings with him: instability and levity lie on the surface.

101 The friendship of a single-minded man is true and honest: but the speech of the deceitful minded is false and unstable.

102 The wicked say one thing with their mouth, and mean another in their heart, nor do

their actions agree with either. But the thoughts, words, and acts of the good are all one."

So Hiranyaka formed a friendship with the Crow, and after having entertained him with the best that he had, returned to his hole. The Crow also returned to his own place again. Some time passed, which the two newly-made friends spent in presents of food, complimentary sayings after each others' health, and confidential conversation. One day the Crow said to Hiranyaka, "My dear friend! this is a very difficult place for a Crow to live in, for there is nothing to eat. Let us go elsewhere." Hiranyaka replied:

103 "Teeth, hair, nails, and men, have no beauty when torn from their proper place: a wise man knowing this will not forsake the position that belongs to him."

"My dear Sir," rejoined the Crow, "this is a cowardly sentiment; for:

104 Lions, brave men, and elephants leave a place (that does not suit them) and go: crows, cowards, and deer stay where they are and perish.

105 What difference is there to a brave man between his own country and a foreign land? Wherever he may go he gains the mastery by the strength of his arm. In whatever forest the lion ranges, armed with teeth and claws, and lashing his tail with rage; there he slakes his thirst in the blood of the lordly elephant that he has slain."

"Besides," said Hiranyaka, "to what place shall we go? For it has been said:

106 With one foot a prudent man moves: with the other he stands still. It is not well to leave one abode till another has been found."

The Crow replied, "I know of a place to which we can go. I have thoroughly examined it. If you will come with me I will show you the way." Hiranyaka said, "Where is it?" The Crow answered, "In the forest of Dandaka is a pond called Karpûragaura; and close by dwells a very old and dear friend of mine, a Tortoise called Manthara; for:

107 To instruct others in wisdom is comparatively easy. A right-minded man will look first to the performance of his own duties.

He will provide us with all sorts of good things to eat and drink." Hiranyaka said, "And what am I to do? I cannot stay here alone; for:

108 It is not right to remain in a place where there is no respect for the good, no work, no friends, and no interest in the search after knowledge.

109 A man with money, a teacher of divine science, a ruler, a river and a physician: where these five things are wanting a home should not be made.

110 Business, fear, modesty, politeness, liberality: where these five things are wanting a home should not be made.

111 Men who pay their debts, a physician, a river

of good water, and a Brâhman versed in the Veda: where these four things are wanting a home should not be made.

Therefore you must take me with you."

The Crow gladly consented, and he started for the pool in company with the Mouse. They beguiled the journey by discoursing on all kinds of profitable subjects, and were at last met by Manthara, who had seen them arriving from a distance. The tortoise respectfully welcomed Laghupatanaka, who introduced Hiranyaka to him. Manthara then conducted them both to his dwelling and treated them with the greatest hospitality; for:

112 Fire is the superior of the twice born: the Brâhman is the superior of the four castes: a husband is the superior of wives, but a visitor takes precedence of all.

"My dear friend Manthara," said the Crow, "may I ask you to be specially attentive to this stranger, for he is a character of the most exalted virtue. He is the very prince of mice. I doubt if even the two thousand tongues of the Serpent king could adequately express his worth." The Crow then related the story of Chitragrîva. When Manthara heard this he saluted Hiranyaka with the utmost respect, and said, "I pray you, my worthy sir, tell me the reason of your choosing to dwell in a lonely forest." Hiranyaka replied, "Most willingly," and related the following story:

STORY V

In a town called Champaka there is a society of mendicant devotees. One of these, whose name was Chûrâkarṇa, used to collect food by begging, and after his meals used to place what remained of the food on a shelf over his head, and go to sleep. On these remnants I used daily to feast. One day a fellow mendicant, called Vînâkarṇa, an intimate friend, came to see him. While they were engaged in conversation upon various subjects, Chûrâkarṇa kept on striking the ground with a cane to frighten me away from the dish. Vînâkarṇa said, "My friend, how is it that you do not listen to me, but seem to be attending to something else ; for :

113 An agreeable countenance: a beaming eye: fondness for converse: a pleasing voice: exceeding kindness: a courteous manner: these are always the marks of a friend.

114 A disagreeable manner: ignoring past kindnesses: want of courtesy: spreading one's failings abroad: forgetting one's name at meeting: these are the signs of a man who is ill disposed."

"My good sir!" answered Chûrâkarṇa, "I am attending to you: but don't you see this mouse is eating up my dinner?" Vînâkarṇa examined the shelf, and said, "How could a diminutive mouse jump up on to this shelf? There must be some cause for this ; for it has been said :

115 When a young wife, for no obvious reason,

keeps on hugging and kissing her old husband, and pulls his hair unmercifully, there must be some motive for it."

Chûrâkarṇa asked what was the meaning of that. Vînâkarṇa said:

STORY VI

In the province of Gaur there is a city called Kauśâmbî, and in it dwelt a rich merchant whose name was Chandanadâsa. Although his age was considerable, he had not ceased to have a hankering after female beauty, and so, his wealth being the principal inducement, he persuaded a certain merchant's daughter called Lîlâvatî, to be the partner of his fortunes. This Lîlâvatî was young and amorous: consequently her somewhat decrepid husband was not much to her taste; for:

116 As the moon is no attraction to those frozen with cold, nor the sun to those scorched by the heat: so the heart of woman is not drawn to a husband worn out with old age.

117 When grey hairs have appeared, what is a man's love worth? He is a mere drug. Women will turn their attention elsewhere.

However, the old husband was desperately in love with his wife; for:

118 Attachment to money, and desire for life are always strong in living beings: but a young wife is dearer to an old man than life itself.

119 A worn-out old man can neither enjoy or relinquish the pleasures of sense. A dog

that has lost his teeth can only lick a bone with his tongue.

Now Lîlâvatî, being an impetuous young woman, disgraced herself and her family by falling in love with the son of a merchant ; for :

120 Independence : living in her father's house : going out to festal gatherings : freely associating with men connections of the family : staying away from home : keeping company with light women : wasting her property : jealousy of other women : these are the causes of a woman's downfall.

121 Drinking : bad company : absence from her husband : gadding about : overmuch sleep : staying in other person's houses : these six things are the ruin of a woman.

122 If there is no place : no opportunity : no male attraction : then indeed the chastity of women is assured.

123 Women care for no one much, and dislike no one much : cattle in a forest are always wandering about in search of fresh pasture.

124 Women have always been inconstant, even among the gods : fortunate indeed are those whose wives keep perfectly faithful.

125 Neither shame—nor sense of propriety—nor decency—nor timidity—none of these things is the reason for a woman's fidelity. The sole reason is the absence of a suitor.

126 A woman is a pot of clarified butter. A man is burning charcoal. It is not prudent to put the butter close to the fire.

127 A father is a woman's guardian in childhood: her husband in youth: her sons in old age: A woman is not fit to take care of herself.

128 It is not well to sit in a secluded spot with a mother, a sister, or a daughter. The senses are powerful, and beguile even the prudent.

One day Lîlâvatî was sitting on a couch with the merchant's son, making love to him She suddenly observed her husband approaching, and, getting up in a great hurry, she rushed forward and kissed him and embraced him with ardour. Her lover took the opportunity meanwhile of escaping; for it is said:

129 All the learning of Usanâ, all the wisdom of Vrihaspati, the whole of it exists by nature in the minds of women.

A bystander, who had seen Lîlâvatî's affectionate greeting to her husband, wondered what the reason might be. His doubts were soon, however, dispelled when he happened to see the lover making off in the distance. Therefore I say: When a young wife, for no obvious reason, keeps on hugging and kissing her old husband, and pulls his hair unmercifully, there must be some motive for it.

"Accumulation of wealth," said the mendicant after a moment's reflection, "must be the motive of this mouse's energy; for:

130 In this world every man who has wealth is powerful: even the power of sovereigns rests upon their wealth."

So the mendicant, continued Hiranyaka, got a

spade, dug open my hole, and seized on the store that I had accumulated. After that, my provisions all being gone, I lost my energy and my courage, and unable to procure any food for myself, I was timidly creeping about when Chûrâkarṇa saw me. He exclaimed :

131 "By means of wealth every one gains power : with wealth every one is wise : Look at this wretched mouse ! he has found his level at last.

132 The schemes of a man who has lost his wealth and his mind come to naught, as brooks are dried up by the heat of summer.

133 The rich man has friends : the rich man has relations : the rich man is of importaṇce : the rich man is learned.

134 The house of a man without a son is empty : The house of one who has no true friend is empty : the whole world is empty to the fool. The poor man is empty of everything.

135 Of poverty or death, poverty is reckoned the worst. The pain of death lasts but a short time—the pain of poverty is unendurable.

136 The senses are not lessened : the intelligence is not destroyed : the speech is still clear : but the man deprived of the warmth of riches is changed in a moment. How wonderful is this !"

Hiranyaka continued :

When I heard that I thought to myself : It is not well for me to stay here, neither is prudent to communicate my intentions to another ; for :

137 A prudent man should not publish to the world the loss of his money: the distress of his mind: evil doings at home: his being cheated: his disgrace.

138 A man should conceal his age: his money: his domestic troubles: his private counsels: the medicine that he takes—his penances: his liberality: his disgrace.

139 When fortune is hostile, and men's efforts are unavailing, how should a wise man find happiness except in the forest?

140 A wise man is quite willing to die, but he will not suffer poverty. A fire may become extinguished, but it will never grow cool.

141 As of a cluster of blossoms, so is the state of a wise man: he may either be an ornament for the head, or he may wither in the forest.

As to go on living in a state of beggary, that is a despicable condition; for:

142 Better that the funeral pile should be kindled with the life of one who has lost his possessions, than that he should be compelled to ask alms of churlish men.

143 Through poverty he comes to shame: overcome with shame he loses his energy: his energy gone he is despised: the contempt of others destroys his self-respect: devoid of self-respect he becomes despondent: sunk in despondency he loses his reason: deprived of reason he goes to destruction. Alas! poverty is the root of all evils.

144 Better a vow of silence than a single unkind word:
Better to be impotent than to approach the wives of others.
Better to cast off life than to take pleasure in the words of a slanderer.
Better to be a beggar than to feast on other men's riches.

145 Better an empty house, than one with a lazy master:
Better a harlot for wife than a woman of good family married before.
Better to dwell in the forest than in a city where is an unjust ruler.
Better self-destruction than association with the wicked.

146 As servitude destroys self-respect: as moonlight darkness: as old age beauty: as discourse about Vishnu and Siva sin: so poverty destroys a hundred virtues.

Since my mind is thus, how could I live upon another's store: surely that would lead to destruction; for:

147 Knowledge only on the surface: love bought for money: food at the expense of another: these are three miseries of men.

148 The life of the sick man: of the man who spends many years in exile: of the man who lives on the charity of another: the man who sleeps in another's house: the life which these men live is but a living death.

I knew all this, but covetousness still impelled me to take the food; for it has been said:

149 Through covetousness reason is dislodged: from covetousness springs greed. The man who is greedy after gain is tormented in this world and in the next.

Vînâkarṇa then struck me a blow with the stick which was in his hand, and I thought to myself:

150 The man greedy after wealth, whose senses are not restrained, is in a state of discontent: all evils are the lot of him who is dissatisfied.

151 The man with a contented mind has abundant riches.
The earth seems as if carpeted with leather to the foot of one who wears a shoe.

152 What peace can those have who are always running after wealth, impelled by avarice, compared with that which calm souls enjoy, satisfied with the nectar of contentment?

153 The man who has read, heard, performed all that the world can give him, hopes nothing and expects nothing.

154 The man is lucky who has not been obliged to hang about the door of the rich—who has never experienced the pain of separation—who has never spoken an idle word.

155 A hundred miles is not far for the man to travel who is greedy after gain: but the contented man cares not overmuch for that which is close at hand.

Therefore it is absolutely necessary for each

man to know what is his position and his duty; for it has been said:

156 What is righteousness? Compassion toward all living beings. What is happiness? To a man in this world freedom from disease. What is kindness? A virtuous disposition. What is learning? Discrimination (between good and bad).

157 When a man is in a difficulty the power of discrimination is learning. Calamities will always be pressing on the heels of those who have no discrimination.

158 For the sake of a family a man should leave a single person; a family for a commune—a commune for a country: but for the sake of his own soul he should abandon the earth.

159 Either water without toil, or luxuries followed by danger. I reflect and I see plainly that where there is tranquillity, there is happiness.

"And so," continued Hiranyaka, "I went to live in a forest—remote and uninhabited; for:

160 If a man has lost his wealth, a forest haunted by tigers and elephants—the trees for a dwelling—fruits and water for food—the grass for a bed—bark for clothing—this is better for him than a dwelling in the midst of his relations.

"Afterwards," said the Mouse, "I was favoured by my friend the Crow with one kindness after another, and now that I have been introduced to your honourable self, and have been lucky enough to add you to the number of my friends, I am indeed exalted to the height of bliss; for:

161 Two fruits, sweet and wholesome, grow upon the poison tree of this world; one of them is delight in poetry with its taste like nectar, the other is the society of the virtuous.

162 Association with one's fellow-men; devotion to Keśava: bathing in the waters of Ganges: these one should look on as the three vital things in this world which passes away."

Then Manthara answered and said:

163 "Riches are but the dust of the feet: youth is the force of the mountain torrent: manhood is as unsteady as a drop of water: life is like the foam of the sea: righteousness alone will unbar the gates of heaven. He who does not perform righteousness, shall be consumed by the fire of remorse when old age and repentance come upon him.

You heaped up riches: this was why evil fell upon you; for:

164 As a waste pipe is the means for carrying off the waters pent up in a tank, so is liberality the means for the preservation of wealth.

165 The miser who buries his hoard in the ground, makes a road before him to the lower regions.

166 He who not regarding his own happiness seeks to heap up money, is only a bearer of burdens for the sake of others, a vessel of affliction to himself.

It has been well said:

167 If we are rich with that which is neither given to us nor enjoyed, we are rich with that which is hidden in the bowels of the earth.

168 He who passes his life without either giving or using the wealth that he has, does not live, though he breathe like a blacksmith's bellows.

169 What good is wealth to him who neither gives nor uses? What good is strength to him who does not resist his enemies? What good are the Sacred Scriptures to him who neglects his religious duties? What use is a soul to him who does not subdue his senses?

170 The property of the miser might as well be in the possession of others; it is merely a possession to him, but if he lose it he is overwhelmed with grief.

171 The miser's wealth does not go to God nor to the Brâhmans, nor to his relations, nor to himself; it is either destroyed by fire, stolen by thieves, or confiscated by the King.

172 A man may give—he may enjoy—he may lose: these are the three ends for which wealth is destined. The third awaits the man who neither gives nor enjoys.

173 Liberality with kindly words: knowledge without pride: bravery with forbearance: wealth with contempt of possessions: these are four excellences hard to find.

store should be laid up, but not too great a

store. See how the jackal of hoarding propensities was killed by a bow."

Hiranyaka said, "How did that come about?"

Manthara related the following story:

STORY VII

There was once a hunter called Bhairava, who lived at Kalyânakaṭaka. One day he was hungry, so taking his bow he went into the Vindhya forest, where he killed a deer. Taking up the deer to carry it home, he saw a boar of enormous size coming towards him. He therefore laid the deer down on the ground and aimed an arrow at the boar. The boar, who was only wounded, made a roar as terrible as the thunderclouds at the destruction of the world, and charged at the hunter. The hunter, unable to avoid the rush, was felled to the ground by a stroke of the boar's tusks, and lay like a tree cut down by an axe; for:

175 Water: fire: poison: the sword: hunger: sickness: the fall from a precipice: any of these causes is sufficient to destroy the life of a living being.

In addition to this, in the scuffle between them a serpent was trodden to death under their feet.

Just at that moment a jackal called Dîrghârava was prowling about in search of something to eat, and came across the hunter, the boar, the deer, and the serpent, all lying dead. He thought to himself: "Here is a piece of luck; a feast ready for me without any trouble; for:

176 As troubles fall unexpectedly on mortals, so

too do pleasures, but I think here destiny is on my side.

Still, however this may be, I shall have enough here to last me for at least three months.

177 The man will last me one month: the deer and the boar will carry me on for two more: the serpent will last me a day. I will begin on the bowstring."

So saying he proceeded to gnaw the string, when all of a sudden the bow, let go by the severing of the string, flew back, pierced Dîrghârava in the breast and killed him. Wherefore I said, A store should be laid up, but not too great a store. Moreover:

178 A rich man's true wealth is that which he gives away, and that which he enjoys: others after he is dead will enjoy his money and the society of his wife.

"So be it," said Hiranyaka; "what is the use of a long discussion on the matter?

179 Men of learning and wisdom do not hanker after the unattainable: they do not grieve over their losses: they are not cast down even in misfortune.

You must always act with courage and energy:

180 A man who is versed in the Sacred Scriptures may for all that be a fool: the truly learned is he who acts wisely. The mere name of a drug will not cure a man of his disease.

181 What profit are wise maxims to a man who shirks even the least trouble? A lamp,

bring it as near as you may, shows nothing to a blind man.

Therefore, my dear friend, be content with your lot: for

182 A man should take pleasures or pains just as they come. They come round one after another like a wheel.

183 As frogs go to the ditch: as birds to the lake full of water: so does every kind of prosperity flow to the man who is filled with energy.

184 Fortune of her own accord takes up her abode with the man who is endowed with energy, who is prompt and ready, who knows how to act, who is not addicted to vice, who is brave, who shows gratitude for kindness.

185 Even without riches a wise man gains a place of honour; even with riches the miser goes to a place of dishonour. How should a dog, though he wear a golden necklace, gain the splendour of the lion? For that is the lion's natural character, and hosts of virtues spring from it.

186 Thou art rich—wilt thou be proud? thou hast lost thy riches—wilt thou be sad? The falls and rising of men are even as a ball tossed up by the hand.

187 The shadow of a cloud: the friendship of the wicked: new corn: women: youth: riches: are only to be enjoyed for a short time.

188 A man should not be over anxious for his livelihood, for that has been provided by the Creator. The teats of the mother supply

nourishment to her child as soon as it is born.

189 He by whom the swans were formed white—by whom the parrots were made green—by whom the varied hues were given to the peacocks—He will give thee thy subsistence.

Hear another secret of the good :

190 The heaping together of riches gives trouble : the loss of them sorrow : abundance of riches leads men to folly. How can riches confer happiness?

191 The absence of desire for everything is better than wealth even for the sake of performing righteous acts : it is better to keep at a distance from mud than to wash it off.

192 As flesh is eaten by the birds in the air, the beasts of prey on the land, by the fish in in the sea, so everywhere is plenty (provided for all).

193 There is always danger to the rich from the King, from water, from fire, from thieves, from their own relatives, just as there is always danger of death to the living.

194 In a life full of trouble, what trouble is greater than this : that a man should fail in the accomplishment of his wish, and yet, that his wish should not cease.

195 Wealth is difficult to acquire : when it has been gained it is kept with difficulty : the loss of what has been acquired is even as death. Therefore a man should not think on wealth.

196 If the thirst for riches were renounced, there

would be no difference between the rich and the poor; but if place be found for it, it gains the mastery over everything.

197 When a man wishes for anything, his desire for it keeps on continually growing: but as soon as the desire ceases he has really gained the object of his wish.

But enough of all this argument; let us pass the time in amusing conversation; for:

198 The friendships of the virtuous end only with death: their differences are easily pacified: their liberality is unbounded."

On hearing this, Laghupatanaka exclaimed:

"Indeed, Manthara! you are an excellent person: you can always be relied upon; for:

199 Good men are always ready to sympathize with good men in misfortune. Elephants are able to drag other elephants out of the mud.

200 A man who appreciates virtue delights in a virtuous man: the man who is not good himself cares nothing for good men. The bee is attracted to the lotus from the forest: not so the frog, though he dwells in the same place.

201 There is only one man—of all men upon earth, who is worthy of praise—the best, the most excellent of men—the man from whose presence the suppliant does not depart rejected, disappointed of his hopes."

In this manner they passed their time, roving about the forest at their pleasure. One day a deer called Chitrânga, which had been startled by an intruder, came and joined them. Manthara, fearing that the cause of Chitrânga's alarm might be following behind him, plunged hastily into the water, Hiranyaka retreated to his hole, and Laghupatanaka flew up to the top of the highest tree in the neighbourhood. The Crow from his point of vantage looked all round, but failed to see anything of an alarming character: so he descended from his tree, and informing his friends, they reassembled out of their several hiding places. "My worthy Chitrânga," said Manthara, "we are delighted to see you! I trust you will make yourself at home, and take whatever you want in the way of meat and drink. Pray look upon the forest as your own private property. But pray tell us what led you to come here?"

Chitrânga replied, "I was terrified at the approach of a hunter, and I have come here to ask you for protection; for:

202 To turn away one who comes asking for protection, through either avarice or fear, is, in the opinion of wise men, a sin equal to the murder of a Brâhman.

Therefore I am come to you to ask for your friendship and help."

Hiranyaka said: "We shall be delighted to receive you here, and to admit you into the circle of our friends; for:

203 There are four kinds of friends: one's own children: a connexion: one lineally descended: and one rescued from calamity.

I beg of you to remain here and to make yourself at home."

The Deer was delighted at this; and having eaten his fill of grass and drunk water to his heart's content, laid himself down to sleep by the side of the pond; for:

204 The water of a well: the shade of a fig-tree: a brunette, and a house built of bricks, should be warm in the winter, and cool in the summer.

Manthara then turned to the Deer and said: "My dear friend! by whom were you alarmed? Do hunters ever come into such a lonely forest as this?"

The Deer replied: "In the country of Kalinga there is a prince called Rukmângada. He is coming on an expedition with a view to subduing some of the neighbouring states, and he is encamped on the River Chandrabhâgâ. There is a report that he is coming here on his way, and means to take up his position close to this lake early to-morrow morning. Therefore, considering the danger there will be to us, we had better make up our minds without any delay to go elsewhere."

Manthara, the tortoise, on hearing this, was very much frightened, and said: "For my part, I shall be off to another lake at once." The Crow and the Deer agreed to this, and said, "By all means."

Hiranyaka, however, having thought the matter over, said: "It is quite true that the best thing for Manthara would be to go to another lake, but how is he going to get there? For:

205 Water is the safest place for animals that live in the water: a fortress for those who dwell

in fortresses : their own ground for beasts of prey : an army is the protection of kings.

It is quite evident, friend Laghupatanaka, if this plan is carried out you will be in the same condition as

206 The son of the merchant who saw his own wife in the arms of a stranger, and felt very unhappy."

The others said, "How was that?" Hiranyaka said :

STORY VIII

In the country of Kânyakubja there is a king called Virasena. He had a son whose name was Tungabala, whom he made his viceroy in a town called Vîrapura. Tungabala was young and good-looking, and besides this enormously rich. One day when he was walking about his town he came across a certain Lâvangavatî, the wife of a merchant's son, and a very comely damsel. Tungabala then and there fell over head and ears in love with her, hurried back to his house, and sent with all speed a female messenger to fetch the object of his attraction ; for :

207 A man remains in the path of virtue, keeps his feelings under control, observes decency, and practises restraint, only so long as his heart is not made the mark for the darts that fall from the eyes of lovely women.

Moreover, the attraction was mutual. Lâvangavatî, from the very first moment of seeing him, fell a victim to Cupid, and had no eyes for any one else. For it has been said :

208 Falsehood, haste, artifice, envy, greediness: want of principle: these are the innate failings of women.

The messenger arrived and delivered herself of her errand. Lâvangavatî answered, "Tungabala has made a great mistake: I am absolutely devoted to my husband, and have no desires beside him; for:

209 She is a true wife who is skilled in managing her house.
She is a true wife who is fruitful in children.
She is a true wife who lives entirely in her lord:
She is a true wife who is faithful to her husband.

210 The beauty of cuckoos is in their voice:
The beauty of women is fidelity to their lords.
The beauty of the ill favoured is knowledge:
The beauty of the religious is patience.

211 She in whom her husband takes no pleasure is not worthy to be called a wife. The heaven is bright above her in whom her husband is well pleased.

Whatever then my lord may order, that I do without any discussion." The messenger replied, "Is that really so?" Lâvangavatî answered, "It is, upon my word." The messenger then went back and told Tungabala exactly what Lâvangavatî had said. Tungabala was distracted with grief and love, and exclaimed, "I cannot possibly live without her!" The female emissary said: "You must get her husband to bring her here, and hand her over to you." Tungabala replied, "But how can that be done?" The woman answered, "You must use stratagem; for it is said:

212 What cannot be done by force, can sometimes be done by stratagem. An elephant that was going along a muddy road was killed by a jackal."

The Prince said: "How was that?"

She related the following:

STORY IX

An Elephant named Karpûratilaka lived in the forest of Brahma. He was the envy of all the jackals in the neighbourhood, and they said among themselves: "If anything were to happen to this beast, we should have enough to live on for four or five months." One of them, an old Jackal of great cunning, said, "I will see what I can do to bring about this result." So he went up to Karpûratilaka, made a humble obeisance, and said: "Noble sir! deign to cast your eyes on me." "And pray who are you?" answered the Elephant, "and where do you come from?" The Jackal replied, "Sir! I am a jackal. The animals of the forest have met together in assembly, and have resolved to choose a ruler. They have chosen you, most noble sir, as endowed with every princely virtue, and they beg to offer you the sovereignty of the forest; for:

213 He who is without fault in the duties pertaining to his family, who is powerful, righteous,

skilled in policy: such a man is fit to be a ruler on earth.

214 First, a king must be procured: then, a wife: then, riches. If there were no king, whence could there be a wife or riches?

215 The cloud is the supporter of all creatures, so is also the king. If the cloud fail it may be possible to live, but not if there be no king.

216 In this world, dependent on external things, man abides in the lot appointed him through fear of punishment. A woman, even of good family, submits to her husband through fear of the rod, even if he be weak, or a cripple, sick, or without wealth.

Therefore, that the auspicious moment for proclaiming your majesty's sovereignty may not pass by, make haste and come with me: I will show you the road." The Elephant then started, but as he was running along the road pointed out by the jackal, in great haste to secure the sovereign power offered him, he fell up to his neck into a bog. "My worthy Jackal," cried the Elephant, "what is to be done now? I am set fast in this bog." The Jackal said, laughing: "If your majesty will have the goodness to take hold of the end of my tail, I will pull you out." Such was she result of trusting in a treacherous person; for it has been said:

217 If you are deprived of the company of good people, you will always be likely to fall among knaves.

So the end of it was that the Elephant, unable to escape from the bog, was eaten by the jackals;

wherefore I say: That which cannot be done by force, may sometimes be done by stratagem.

Tungabala then, by the woman's advice, took the merchant's son, whose name was Chârudatta, into his service, and he was employed by the Prince on all matters of importance. The Prince one day said to Chârudatta—still under the woman's advice—"I have a vow to perform to Gaurî for a month. Bring me therefore every day a woman of good family, so that we may duly perform the sacred rites together." Chârudatta did as he was ordered, and having procured such a woman as the Prince desired, hid himself to see what would happen next. The lady was duly presented to the Prince, who did homage to her at a respectful distance with great ceremony, and having presented her with gold, jewels and perfume, sent her away in the care of a guard. Chârudatta on seeing this from his hiding place felt quite satisfied, and attracted by the gold and the jewels, he presented his own wife the next day, and hid himself as before. What happened was, however, quite different, for Tungabala, recognizing Lâvangavatî, the delight of his heart, so far from keeping her at a distance, lavished upon her all kinds of caresses, and at last lay down upon the couch with her. Chârudatta, seeing all this, was struck dumb with astonishment, and not knowing in the least what to do was overwhelmed with grief.

"And this will be your fate," said Hiranyaka to the Crow, concluding his story.

Manthara, however, was too frightened to pay any attention to the tale, and started off in the utmost hurry, followed by Hiranyaka and the others. Soon after they had started, Manthara was caught by a hunter, who tied him up in a bag and set off home, blessing his good luck.

The Deer, the Mouse, and the Crow followed at a distance, overwhelmed with grief. Hiranyaka exclaimed:

218 "I have reached the end of one sorrow, as it were the furthest shore of the sea, and now a second has overtaken me. For my sins troubles have been multiplied upon me.

219 A friend who is really a friend may be gained in good fortune: but if his friendship is unfeigned he will not fail in adversity.

220 Not in a mother, not in a wife, not in a brother, not in a son, are men so confident as in a friend who is of like disposition to themselves."

Thus continually reflecting, he exclaimed:

"Ah! how adverse is my fate; for:

221 The various states of which I have been a partaker from time to time in this world—some good and some bad—are the result of my own actions in a former life.

222 The body vanishes: wealth is the root of misfortunes: union only ends in separation: everything that comes into being passes away."

He thought again within himself, and then he said:

223 "Who was the creator of this word of two syllables, MITRAM: the preserver from enemies, danger, and grief, the haven of peace and love?

224 A friend who is the elixir of love to the eyes, the joy of the heart, a vessel of sympathy whether in pleasure or pain, is hardly to be found. Others—filled with the hope of gain—friends in prosperity—these abound everywhere.

Truly misfortune is the touchstone of friendship."

Hiranyaka, full of grief and lamentation, said to Laghupatanaka and Chitrânga, "We must try and get Manthara out of this difficulty before the hunter leaves the forest." They answered both at once: "Well! tell us what you think would be the best thing to do." Hiranyaka replied, "Chitrânga should go near the water and lie down pretending to be dead, and Laghupatanaka must stand over him and peck at him with his beak. The hunter, who is very fond of venison, is certain to leave the Tortoise and go after the Deer; while he is gone I will gnaw the strings by which Manthara is tied up, and let him out." They did exactly what Hiranyaka had advised. The hunter, tired with his chase, was sitting under a tree and saw the Deer in the position which the Mouse had suggested. He immediately left the Tortoise on the edge of the pond, and taking his hunting knife in his hand ran off to secure the Deer. Meanwhile Hiranyaka set to work, used his teeth to some purpose, and let Manthara out of his prison;

the Tortoise then scuttled down the bank into the water, while the Deer jumped up and ran away before the hunter had time to reach him. The hunter then, disappointed of his venison, returned to the tree, and found the bag empty and the Tortoise gone. "This," he said, "serves me right for not acting with due consideration ; for :

225 The man who throws away a certainty and pursues an uncertainty, loses everything. For we can be sure of nothing till we have got it."

So the hunter had to go home without any supper, and Manthara with his friends went back to their own place and lived happily together for the rest of their lives.

Then the Princes said, delighted with the stories : "Our interest in what you have told us is overwhelming : we have learned our lesson."

Vishṇuśarman replied : "So far your desires have been granted ; moreover :

226 May good men never want a friend : may plenty be the lot of all men. May princes, ever performing their own duties, protect the earth. May your prudent counsel live, like a newly-married bride, to gladden the minds of the virtuous. And may that deity whose crest-jewel is the new moon, grant unto men prosperity."

END OF MITRALÂBHA

THE FORMING OF FRIENDSHIP

II

SUHRIDBHEDA

SEPARATION OF FRIENDS

SUHRIDḆHEDA

SEPARATION OF FRIENDS

SOON after this the Princes said to Vishṇuśarman :

" Sir ! you have taught us how friendships should be formed : we should now like to hear how they may be broken."

Vishṇuśarman replied :

" Then I will instruct you in the separation of friends, and on this subject the first verse is :

1 A lion and a bull lived in a forest and were great friends : but their friendship, which kept on increasing, was destroyed by a greedy mischievous jackal."

" And pray how was that ? " said the Princes.

Vishṇuśarman related the following story :

STORY I

There is a city in Dakshinapatha called Suvarnavatî, and in it lived a very rich merchant whose name was Vardhamâna. Now although he had more money than he knew what to do with, some of his relations in the town were as rich as himself, and so he thought he ought to try and add something to his hoard.

2 A man's greatness is increased when he looks down upon some one lower than himself, but those who are always looking above themselves are insignificant.

3 Even a murderer of Brâhmans is respected if he is rich. A man may be descended from the Moon, but if he is poor he is an object of contempt.

4 Fortune will not lavish her favours on a man who has no enterprise, who is idle, slack, trusting everything to fate, any more than a lively young wife cares to embrace an old husband.

5 Idleness, fondness for women, bad health, home-sickness, self-satisfaction—these are the six obstacles to greatness.

6 He who having but little wealth fancies himself rich—I think the Creator, who does all things well, will not increase that which he has.

7 A son incapable of endurance—giving no pleasure to his friends—cowardly—the laughing-stock of his enemies—may no woman ever bear such a son as this.

8 A man should try to gain wealth : when he has gained it he should take care of it : what he has lawfully gained he should increase : and he should spend liberally at sacred places of pilgrimage.

If wealth be not added to, however small your expenditure, it will waste away like ointment. If it is not enjoyed, it is unprofitable.

9 On the one hand is the ointment which melts

away: on the other the ever increasing store of the Ant. Seeing this, a man should make every day fruitful in liberality, study, and good works.

10 By drops of water a pitcher is filled. So is it with religion, wealth, and all good actions.

Such sentiments as these filled Vardhamânas' mind. He therefore harnessed two bulls to his cart—one called Sanjîvaka, the other Nandaka; and loading it with all kinds of wares started to trade in Kashmîr; for:

11 What load is too heavy for the strong man?
What work is too hard for the man of energy?
What country is strange to the man who has knowledge?
How can a man feel himself to be a stranger among those who speak friendly?

While they were on their journey, Sanjîvaka fell down in the forest of Durga and broke his knees. Vardhamâna seeing this, thought to himself:

12 A skilful man may carry on his business where he will: the end will be what the Creator has ordained.

13 A man should never be dismayed; for in keeping up good courage, the success of every enterprise is assured.

Fortified with these reflections, Vardhamâna unharnessed Sanjîvaka from the cart and went on his journey; and the ox, getting along as best he could on three legs remained behind.

14 The allotted term of life will save a man from

vital injury, even if he be bitten by a deadly serpent—plunged in the sea—or fall from a high mountain.

15 If his time has not come, a man does not die, even if pierced by a hundred arrows: but if his time has come he will not live, though pricked only by a blade of grass.

16 What is protected by fate stands, though it be not cared for; what is doomed by fate falls, though carefully guarded. One man though lost in a trackless forest lives: another, safe at home, all the care in the world will not keep alive.

As time went on, Sanjîvaka, wandering about the forest and picking up a good living, grew fat, and set up a cheerful bellowing. It so happened that in this very same forest there lived a lion called Pingalaka, whose strength and ferocity had for some time secured him the mastery over all the other inhabitants of the forest.

As it has been said:

17 No anointing or religious rites are performed by the beasts for the lion: the sovereignty naturally belongs to him who has gained the kingdom by his power.

One day Pingalaka, being thirsty, went to the banks of the Jumna to drink, and heard the bellowing of Sanjîvaka, which seemed to him like the roar of the thunderclouds at the destruction of the world. He was so frightened that he forgot all about his thirst, and ran away back to his den, without drinking, where he stood trembling, and wondering what on earth the noise meant. Two jackals—Karataka and Damanaka—the sons of his minister, came by, and finding him in this state, said one to the other, "What is the meaning of this? Here is our lord and master; he went to the river to drink, and has come back without drinking anything at all." Said the other, "My service is not much to my taste, so I certainly shall not stand about here to see what he wants; all the reward that I get for my fidelity is to be passed over and slighted by our master.

18 See what people do who make their living out of service: they have to sacrifice their independence.

19 Those who are at the beck and call of others must endure heat, cold, wind, fatigue. With half the amount of the toil they have to go through, a wise man, performing penance, would be satisfied.

20 Life is agreeable or disagreeable exactly in proportion to the dependence or independence of each person. If those who are dependent on others are alive, no one is dead.

21 'Come—go—stoop down—rise up—speak—hold your tongue.' This is the way rich men order the needy about, who are held fast in the grasp of what they hope to gain.

22 Foolish persons, desirous of gain, are like harlots. They are continually adorning themselves that they may be the instrument for some one else's pleasure.

23 Servants who humbly obey even their master's

glances are those whom he looks on with favour. A master's glances are always uncertain.

24 The servant bows down for the sake of rising: he throws away his life for the sake of living: he suffers pain for the sake of pleasure. What fool is greater than a servant?

25 If he is silent, he is a fool. If he talks freely, he is a chatterer. If he is submissive, he is timid. If he is impatient, he is ill-mannered. If he keeps close by his master's side, he is a bore. If he remains at a distance, he is never to be found when he is wanted. The duties of servitude are exceedingly difficult—impossible to be duly performed, even by one possessed of superhuman powers."

When Karataka had delivered himself of these maxims, Damanaka said: "My dear brother! Such ideas as these should never enter your head. What do you mean:

26 Are not these mighty lords to be served with all devotion, who, as a reward for our service, will after no long time fulfil all our desires?

27 The chariot, the elephant, the horse, the white parasol with its lofty pole, the tall chowries—how are these honours to be gained without the toils of service?"

"All this may be true enough," replied Karataka; "what has it to do with us? It is never wise to meddle in other people's business.

28 The man who interferes in other people's

business will get into difficulties over it, as
the monkey did who pulled out the wedge."

"How was that?" asked Damanaka. Karataka said:

STORY II

A certain writer named Śubhadatta was building a music-hall on a piece of ground in Magadeśa, near the forest of Dharma. The carpenters had been sawing a piece of wood down the middle, and had left it partly open by putting in a wedge. After the carpenters had left their work, a number of monkeys who lived in the forest came to the place, and one of them, under the guidance of an evil fate, sat down on the piece of wood, and taking hold of the wedge tried to pull it out. At last, after some difficulty, he managed get the wedge out, when the two pieces of wood came together and held him fast, so that he perished. Therefore I say: The man who interferes in other people's business will certainly get into difficulties.

"Very true," replied Damanaka, "but it *is* a servant's business to look after his master's interests." "That," returned Karataka, "is the Prime Minister's business; you had better leave it to him. Persons of inferior position should never meddle with the affairs of those above them.

29 He who takes upon himself the duties of
another, with the desire of doing good to his
master, will be sorry for it, as the ass was
who was beaten for braying."

"How was that?" said Damanaka. Karataka related the following story:

STORY III

In Vârâṇasî there is a washerman named Karpurapata. One day, tired out with sport, he fell asleep. Meanwhile, some thieves entered the house with the intention of carrying off his money. An Ass was tied up in the courtyard, and in the same place a Dog was sitting.

The Ass, seeing the thieves, said to the Dog: "Why don't you wake your master up? It is your business." The Dog replied: "You need not trouble about that. You know perfectly well that though I guard our master's house, he takes no trouble to reward my services: in fact, he is even very irregular in giving me my allowance of food. Masters are apt to become very remiss in the duty they owe to the servants, as long as everything goes on quietly." The Ass replied: "Listen to me, you rascal:

30 He who at the time of work asks for payment, what kind of a friend, or what kind of a servant do you think he is?"

The Dog answered: "He who does not pay his servants for the work done, what sort of a master do you think he is?

31 The maintenance of dependents: the service due to a master: the performance of righteousness: the begetting of a son: these things cannot be performed by deputy."

The Ass replied with anger: "Wretch that you are who would neglect the duty you owe to our master! Well! I will see what I can do to wake him up; for:

32 With the back one should worship the Sun : with the belly, fire : a master should be served with all one's powers : the next world should be sought by freedom from deceit."

With these words the Ass set up a loud braying. The washerman, woke up by the noise, was very angry, and beat the Ass so violently that the unfortunate animal died. Wherefore I say : He who takes upon himself the duties of others with the desire of doing good to his master, will be sorry for it.

"We," continued Karataka, "have our appointed duty, and that is hunting ; I think we had better stick to that." After a short pause he added, "And I don't know that we need trouble much about even that to-day, since there is plenty over from yesterday's meal, and the scraps can be eaten up first." Damanaka answered angrily : "Do you mean to say that you serve the king only for what you expect to get out of him ? It is ridiculous for a servant to say that ; for :

33 A wise man desires the alliance of a king for the sake of helping his friends and harming his enemies. Any one (even an ignorant man) may live to pamper his own appetite.

34 The man on whom depends the life of Brâhmans, friends, relations, he indeed has true life. Any one may live for themselves.

35 May he live long who, while he lives, is the life of many. Is it not the crow who fills his own crop with his beak ?

36 One man goes into servitude for five farthings,

another—and a man of wisdom—for an enormous sum of money. Another is not attracted even by a sum as large as that.

37 Since men are equal by birth, how degrading is service! How can the man be said to live who does not stand first?

It has been said :—

38 There is a great difference between a horse, an elephant, and iron—between wood, stone, and cloth—between women, men, and water.

39 When a dog finds a greasy dirty bone, with all the meat gone, and only a piece or two of skin hanging on to it, he is delighted, though it does not satisfy his hunger; but the lion letting the jackal go out of his grasp, slays the elephant. Every one when he is in difficulties desires a result in accordance with his natural disposition."

"Then, again," said Karataka, "you must consider what a difference there is between the servant and his master.

40 The dog wags his tail, and lies on the ground upon his back before any one who will give him a mouthful. The lordly elephant looks on gravely, and only eats after a hundred flattering entreaties.

41 Man may live very few years on earth, but if that short time is passed with honour, associated with knowledge, strength, and glory—that wise men call life. The crow which eats the sacred offerings lives for a hundred years.

42 A man who cannot distinguish between good

and evil—with whom those who know the sacred ordinances will have nothing to do—whose only desire is to fill his belly—what difference is there between a beast-like man such as this and a beast?"

"But you must recollect," rejoined Karataka, "that we are only subordinates; what have we to do with such exalted sentiments?" Damanaka replied: "How long does it take a minister to gain supremacy? or how long does he remain a subordinate? for:

43 No one for his own natural disposition is honoured or dishonoured. In this world honour or dishonour is gained by men as the result of their own acts.

44 Just as a large stone is carried up hill with difficulty, but rolls down again in a moment, so it is with the soul of man with regard to virtue and vice.

Therefore the soul of every man is dependent on the man's own efforts.

45 By his own actions a man falls or rises. As the digger of a well or the builder of a wall."

"But what," said Karataka, "do you mean by all this?" "Here is our lord and master, Pingalaka," answered Damanaka; "he started for the river to drink some water, and frightened by something he turned back again and came home." "And how do you know that?" said Karataka. "A wise man," returned Damanaka, "knows everything; for:

46 Even beasts understand what is said. Horses

and elephants, if they are told to go on, obey. The wise man guesses the meaning of that which lives only in thought. The keen intellect can grasp that which has only been hinted.

47 By the appearance—by the gestures—by the gait—by the movement—by the speech—by the changes of the eye or of the mouth: by these things the inmost thoughts of a man are discerned.

So," concluded Damanaka, "I will take advantage of the state of alarm in which our master is, and by my superior wisdom I will get him into my power.

48 He who knows how to speak opportunely—to show kindness proportioned to its object—whose anger is according to his strength—he is a wise man."

"My dear friend," said Karataka, "you are totally ignorant of the elements of service; just observe this:

49 He who comes without being called: he who speaks without being spoken to: he who thinks himself of any value to his master: that servant is stupid."

"How can I be ignorant of service?" replied Damanaka.

50 "Is anything of itself beautiful or not beautiful? What pleases any man—to him that is beautiful.

51 An intelligent man will study the disposition of every individual: when he has found it out

he will insinuate himself into that person's favour.

52 If he is called, he should say at once, 'Here I am! command me.' And he should carry out his master's orders to the best of his ability.

53 He whose desires are moderate—who is firm, wise—who follows his master like his shadow —who does all his bidding without delay— that man may live in a king's palace."

"Sometimes," continued Karataka, "our master is displeased with you for going to him at unseasonable hours." "Perhaps," answered Damanaka. "Still, close attendance on his master is a servant's duty; for:

54 It is the mark of a weak man to do nothing for fear of making mistakes. People do not abstain from eating for fear of indigestion.

55 A prince favours the man who is near him, even if he be destitute of learning—of low family—clownish. Princes, women, and creepers generally wind themselves round what is nearest."

"Well," said Karataka, "and when you have reached our master, what do you mean to say?" "I shall first of all try and find out," answered Damanaka, "whether he is well disposed to me or not." "How are you going to do that?" said Karataka. Damanaka replied: "The signs are these:

56 Looking towards a servant from a distance, a pleasant smile in giving orders, praise in one's absence, calling to mind agreeable subjects;

57 Courtesy towards a servant, liberality, increasing his pleasures, admission of good intentions when one has made a mistake. These are the signs of a kindly disposed master.

58 Taking up one's time unreasonably, raising hopes that are not fulfilled, withholding rewards. A sensible man will know that these are the signs of an evil-disposed master.

When I have found this out to my satisfaction," continued Damanaka, "I shall address him in such a way that he will do what I want.

59 Wise men have taught us that incapacity is the cause of misfortune: that skill in expedients leads to prosperity: that success or failure comes to each man, according to his own knowledge and discretion.

60 With a kind master faults are virtues: with a severe master virtues are faults: with a just master faults are faults, and virtues are virtues. There are masters of these three classes."

Karataka answered, "True, but until a seasonable opportunity arise, you ought not to speak; for:

61 Even if Vrihaspati were to speak a word out of season, he would be looked on as devoid of understanding, and he would incur eternal disgrace."

"My good friend," replied Damanaka, "you need not alarm yourself: I will take care not to say anything that is not to the point; for:

62 When danger is impending, when the road is lost, when the time for action is passing

rapidly—then a servant who wishes his master well ought to speak, bidden or unbidden.

If I do not offer such advice as is suitable to the occasion, I shall fail in my duty to our master.

63 The attainments by means of which a man makes his living, and for which he is commended by good men, should always be preserved and improved by their owner.

Therefore," concluded Damanaka, "I pray of you to approve my visit to Pingalaka." Karataka replied: "So be it, then; and may good luck attend you.

64 Go, and may you gain wealth—may you be prosperous and fortunate—may you gain the victory over your enemies, and may you return in safety and honour."

Damanaka, dismissed with this benediction, started to visit Pingalaka. The Lion saw him while he was a good way off, and courteously signed to him to come nearer: the Jackal therefore approached, and making a profound reverence, sat himself down. The king said: "It is some time since I have had the pleasure of seeing you." Damanaka replied: "Your Majesty has no need of me as a servant: still, since I thought the occasion was suitable, I have ventured to come before you.

65 Great princes, O mighty sovereign, have need of a straw wherewith to rub their teeth, or to scratch their ears. How much more of a man endowed with hands, head, and voice?

And though, through my long absence, it might seem that my feelings towards your Majesty had become slack, yet this is not so.

66 A jewel may be worn on the foot, a piece of glass on the head: but if it is a question of their value in the market, glass is glass, and a jewel is a jewel.

67 A man of constant mind does not change his nature. Such a change as that would be false. The flame of a torch, though it may have been turned upside down, never goes downwards.

It is absolutely essential that a master should be able to discriminate; for:

68 When a sovereign treats all his subjects exactly alike, without any difference, then the powers which they have for work are destroyed.

69 Men, O king, are of three kinds—very good, very bad, and of a state between the two. A king should therefore employ them on the three kinds of work suitable to them.

70 Servants and ornaments should be used in their proper places. A crest jewel is not worn on the feet, nor an ankle ornament on the head.

71 If a jewel, worthy of being set in gold, have a setting of lead, it does not tinkle nor is it resplendent. But the fault is in the jeweller.

72 If glass be set in a crown, and a jewel in a foot ornament, the fault is not in the jewel, but in the ignorance of the good man who set it.

73 'This is an intelligent man: this one is attached: this man has both qualities.' The king who can appreciate servants in this way will have no lack of faithful followers.

74 A horse, a weapon, a book, a lute, speech, a man, a woman: these things are useful or useless in proportion as their owners are capable of using them.

75 What advantage is to be gained from a faithful servant, but who has no ability? what from an able servant who is hostile? I, O king, am both devoted and able, therefore you ought to make use of my services.

76 If the king despise his servants, they will lapse into a state of stupidity: and intelligent men will then not go near their sovereign because, through the lack of able ministers, he lacks power. When the kingdom is deserted by men of wisdom, sound policy is impossible: when the policy is unsound, the whole country falls into a state of anarchy.

77 The man respected by the sovereign is respected by the people: the man who is degraded by the ruler is despised by all.

78 The wise will welcome a suggestion to the purpose, even from a child: when the sun disappears, is not the light of a lamp to be welcomed?"

Pingalaka said: "My good Damanaka, pray tell me how is it that you, the son of our chief minister, have been so long without coming near us? I doubt not some slanderous talk has influenced you. Pray, speak your mind freely to me." "If it so please your Majesty, may I first be allowed to ask you one question: Why did you, when you had gone to the river for water, come back without drinking, looking as if you had been alarmed in some way or other?" "A very fair question," answered Pingalaka; "and there is no one to whom I could trust the answer, excepting yourself; for I think you are loyal and honest. So I will tell you what you want to know. The truth is, that there is some strange beast in this forest, of a kind that has never been heard of before; it will be necessary for me to leave the place. Did you not yourself hear the terrible noise which gave me so much alarm? Judging from his voice, this animal must be most formidable." "This indeed, Sire," answered Damanaka, "is a very sufficient cause for alarm. I heard the noise as well. But no minister, worth anything, would advise a sovereign to abdicate his throne on the spur of the moment, without first considering whether the danger might not be repelled. Besides, in a matter like this, the ability of your Majesty's servants may have some weight; for:

79 Misfortune acts like a touchstone: from it a man may discover the vigour and intellect not only of his ministers, his wife and his relations, but also of himself."

"My dear friend," said the Lion, "I am terribly alarmed." Damanaka thought to himself: "This is quite obvious, or he would not talk of resigning the sovereignty and going away." So he replied: "Sir! you need have no fear as long as I live. The best thing to do would be to invite Karataka and the rest of your servants to combine, with a view of taking measures to resist the impending dangers, though it may be that it will be a little difficult to secure a combination." The Lion assented to the proposal, and dismissed Karataka and Damanaka with a magnificent present. As they were on the road, Karataka said: "It seems to me, Damanaka, that at present we don't know what this danger is of which the king speaks, nor whether it can be averted or not; and yet we have received a present from him. How can we accept a gift from any one without having done something for it? especially from a king; for:

80 He in whose favour dwells fortune, in whose might dwells victory, in whose anger is death —surely he must be altogether glorious.

81 A sovereign, though he be a child, must not be thought of as a mortal. He is a mighty deity in the form of man.

Damanaka laughed and answered: "My dear friend! you need not trouble yourself. The cause of all this alarm is not far to seek; I knew all along what it was. It was only the bellowing of a bull; and you know bulls are food for us—how much more for a lion!" "Then why," said Karataka, "did you not tell our master so at once?" "And if I had," answered Damanaka, "where would our present have been? Besides:

82 Servants never ought to dispel their master's

fears. A servant who acts in that way would be like Dadhikarṇa."

"How was that?" said Kanataka.

Damanaka related the following story:

STORY IV

In the north country there is a mountain called Arbuda Śikhara, and on it dwelt a lion whose name was Mahâvikrama. As he lay asleep in his den his mane was nibbled by a mouse. He grew very angry at this, for it woke him up, and he tried to catch the mouse, but he could not succeed in doing so, for the mouse escaped into its hole. The lion was at a loss to know what to do, and he said to himself: "There is a saying which tell us:

83 If a man has an insignificant enemy who cannot be overcome by force, an opponent of corresponding power must be put forward to seize him."

The lion, acting on these reflections, went to a neighbouring village where a cat lived called, Dadhikarna, and by presents and promises of all kinds of dainties, he persuaded the cat with some difficulty to come back with him to his cave. After that, the lion had peace and quiet, and slept in comfort, for the mouse never dared venture out through fear of the cat. The lion, however, sometimes heard the mouse in his hole, and on these occasions he would be moved to show still further liberality to the cat. It so happened that one day the mouse, who from his imprisoned condition was absolutely famishing, ventured out to try and get something to eat. That cat caught sight of him, pounced upon him and ate him up. So the lion heard no more of the mouse, and as the cause of his alarm was removed he gradually ceased making any presents to the cat. The end of it was that the cat died of starvation. Therefore I say, Servants ought not to dispel their master's fears.

Damanaka and Karataka then went to Sanjîvaka. Karataka solemnly took up his position at the foot of a tree, while Damanaka went up to Sanjîvaka, and said: "Sir! His Majesty Pingalaka has placed the guardianship of this forest in my hands. Karataka, the general of the host, bids me say, "Come at once, or depart out of this forest without delay. If you disobey, the consequences to you may be very serious, for I know not what my master, who is much enraged with you, may do." Sanjîvaka, who was quite ignorant as to who or what is enemy might be, was terrified at this message, came up to Karataka as he was bid, and saluted him with the profoundest reverence; for as it is said:

84 "Reason is stronger than force." So say the drums which the driver sounds in the elephant's ears: they tell the elephant what his condition is.

Sanjîvaka, filled with alarm, said to Karataka: "General! tell me what I must do." Karataka replied: "If you wish to remain in this forest, you must go and make a humble submission to our sovereign lord." Sanjîvaka replied: "Promise me that I shall return in safety and I will go." Karataka said: "You need have no fears on this point:

85 To the curses of the king of Chedi, Kesava condescended no answer: The lion re-echoes the roar of the thundercloud, not the yell of the jackal.

86 The hurricane tears not up the lowly bending blade of grass. It uproots the lofty trees. The mighty spends his force on the mighty."

Damanaka and Karataka then returned to Pingalaka, and having saluted the king, sat down. "Well, has he been seen?" asked the king. "Sir," replied Damanaka, "we have seen him. What your Majesty has informed us is quite true. The sound proceed from a beast of most enormous strength and alarming appearance. He desires an interview, and your Majesty must therefore be duly prepared. Still, it is not right to be afraid of a mere sound; for:

87 An embankment is broken down by the flowing of water, and a secret council may leak out. By tale bearing friendship is destroyed, and a coward is terrified at the sound of words.

88 Of a mere sound one should not be afraid, not knowing whence the sound proceeds. A harlot, by discovering the cause of a sound, regained her character."

The king said: "How did that come about?" Damanaka related the following story:

STORY V

There is a town named Brahmapura in the Śrîparvata mountains. It was commonly reported there that the top of the mountain was haunted by an evil spirit called Ghantâkarṇa. The truth was that a thief, who had stolen a bell, had been caught and killed by a tiger as he was making his escape with the plunder. The bell had fallen from his hand, and was found by some monkeys, who picked it up and kept on ringing it. Now it was known that the man had been devoured by the tiger, and at the same time the ringing of the bell was heard, so the people concluded that the demon was devouring men and ringing his bell. They therefore all fled from the town. A woman of bad reputation called Karâlâ, who had a little more sense than the rest of her fellow townsmen, set to work and found out the reason for the sound of the bell. So she went to the prince who ruled the town, and said: "Sir! for a trifling remuneration I think I could settle this demon Ghantâkarṇa." The prince, delighted at the suggestion, paid her what she asked. She then, having performed certain religious and magical rites, started for the mountain, and took with her such fruits as she knew monkeys were fond of. On arriving on the scene she strewed the fruits about. Directly the monkeys saw the fruits they dropped the bell and pounced upon the fruits. Karâlâ promptly picked up the bell and returned with it to the town, when she was received with the greatest respect and admiration. Therefore

I say: Of a mere sound one should not be afraid, not knowing whence the sound proceeds.

When Damanaka had finished his story the two jackals went back, brought in Sanjîvaka, and introduced him to the Lion, with whom he lived for a long time on most friendly terms.

One day one of the Lion's brothers, whose name was Stabdhakarna, came on a visit. Pingalaka, having received him hospitably, and entertained him, was starting out on a sporting expedition. Sanjîvaka, seeing this, observed: "Where, your Majesty, is the deer that was killed to-day?" The king replied: "I suppose Damanaka and Karataka know." "Well," said Sanjîvaka, "it would be well to ask them whether there is any over or not." "There is none then," said the Lion, laughing. "What!" exclaimed Sanjîvaka in astonishment, "have those two jackals eaten the whole of it up?" "Eaten—given away and wasted—that is what happens every day," replied the Lion. "And is this done without your Majesty's knowledge and consent," continued Sanjîvaka. "Certainly it is," replied the king. "That," said Sanjîvaka, "is absurd; for it has been said:

89 Nothing should ever be done by a servant without first informing his master, except it be for the warding off of some calamity.

90 A minister should be like a jug, pouring forth little, holding much. He who says, 'What matters time,' is a fool. He who says, 'What signifies a farthing,' is a poor man.

91 He is the best minister who increases the treasury if it be only by one halfpenny. The treasury of one who has a treasury is his life: his life does not consist only in his breath.

92 A man who has lost his wealth will not gain respect even if he observe all the duties of his caste. Deprived of wealth he is deserted even by his wife, how much more by others?

This is a capital fault in the government of a kingdom; for:

93 Extravagance, want of care, accumulation of funds by means of injustice: pilfering, living at a distance: these are said to be the ruin of the treasury.

94 The man who without consideration recklessly squanders his property, will come to beggary, though he be as rich as Kuvera."

Stabdhakarna, hearing Sanjîvaka's remarks, observed: "Damanaka and Karataka have been some time in your service, and they look after matters concerned with peace and war. Now it seems to me that a minister in these departments ought not to have any control over the treasury. There is a good deal to be said on this subject, I will give you the advantage of what I have heard.

95 It is not advisable to place Brâhmans, soldiers, or relations at the head of affairs. A Brâhman, though you may torture him, will not hand over money that is due.

96 When a soldier is employed in a business the first thing he does is to draw the sword:

a relation, on the strength of his relationship, devours everything.

97 An old servant who fills a post makes mistakes, but cares nothing for making them. He despises his master and goes on his course uncontrolled.

98 A servant who has been invested with authority for his good service does not consider himself capable of committing a fault. He thinks his services are everything, and plunders in all directions.

99 A minister, who is made the king's associate and friend in private, is apt to play the king himself. From familiarity he is led on to contempt.

100 A man whose mind is corrupt will be the doer of every evil if he have patience and perseverance enough. Śakuni and Sakaṭara are a proof of this.

101 A minister who is well off will invariably be unmanageable. According to wise men, prosperity and riches always pervert the mind.

102 Not securing advantages that have been gained: wasting his master's money: always giving way: carelessness: deficiency of judgment: addiction to pleasure: these are the faults of a minister.

103 Confiscation of a minister's property: continual inspection: promotion in office: change of employment: this should be the policy of sovereigns towards their ministers.

104 Ministers are something like obstinate tumours: without being squeezed, they will not disgorge the king's treasure.

105 Ministers should frequently have it impressed upon them that they are only the receptacles for the the king's treasure. Will a bathing-dress give out all its water if it is wrung out only once?

Knowing all this," continued Stabdhakarna, "one ought to act as the opportunity demands." "True enough," replied Pingalaka, "but these two jackals are not obedient to my orders." "That," rejoined Stabdhakarna, "is altogether wrong; for:

106 A king should not even allow his own children to be disobedient. Is there not some difference between a real king and a king in a picture?

107 The renown of a paralytic vanishes: the friendship of a wicked man fails: the family of one who has lost his senses comes to nought: the righteousness of one intent on gain is destroyed: knowledge is darkened in one given to vice: the miser has no peace: the kingdom of a ruler who has a careless minister goes to ruin.

108 A king should protect his subjects like a father, from thieves, from government officials, from enemies, from the royal favourites, and from his own covetousness.

"My dear brother," continued Stabdhakarna, "you had much better take my advice. We have all made our meal for to-day, so we need not trouble about any more food. I should advise you to appoint Sanjîvaka to superintend the commissariat; he eats grain, and would not be likely to cheat you." Pingalaka thought it a good plan, and throwing over all his other ministers, appointed Sanjîvaka as his brother had suggested. Damanaka and Karataka very soon found out that their share of provisions was beginning to run short, and they consulted together as to what had better be done. "This is a nice state of things!" said Damanaka. "However, it is no use lamenting over it, for it is all our own fault. According to the story:

109 I have suffered because I touched Svarnarekhâ: the confidante suffered for having bound herself: and the merchant for having tried to get hold of the jewel.

In each case it was all their own fault."

"What is the meaning of that?" said Karataka.

Damanaka replied as follows:

STORY VI

There is a city called Kânchanapura whose ruler was named Vîravikrama. One day his officers of justice were carrying off a certain barber to the place of execution, when a wandering mendicant, called Kandarpaketu, accompanied by a merchant, came forward, and seizing the skirt of the chief officer's robe, exclaimed, "This man must not be punished." "And pray why not?" said the officer. "Hear what I have to say," replied Kandarpaketu, and repeated the verse of which you have asked me the meaning. The officers demanded an explanation of these words, and the wandering mendicant told them the following story. He said: "I am Kandarpaketu, the son of Jîmûtaketu, king of Singhaladvîpa. One day I was in the garden of the palace, when I met a merchant who had just returned from a voyage, and he told me that on the fourteenth day of the month, when he was crossing the ocean, he had seen what appeared to him to be a Kalpa tree in the midst of the waters. That he had approached it, and saw a damsel as beautiful as Lakshmî, the Goddess of Fortune, seated under the tree, decked with all kinds of magnificent jewels, playing on a lute. I therefore took the merchant for my guide and went with him to the place of which he had told me. When we reached it I saw all exactly as he had said, and overcome by the exquisite beauty of the damsel, I plunged into the sea. I immediately found myself in a city of gold, and saw a maiden in a palace of gold reclining on a jewelled couch attended by nymphs. As soon as she saw me she sent one of her attendants inviting me to approach. I asked who the beautiful damsel was, and the attendant replied: 'This is Ratnamanjari, daughter of Kandarpakelî, the king of the Vidyâdharas. She has made a vow to marry the first man who visits the golden city.' I was quite content to accept the omen, and we were immediately married, after which I remained there for some time, quite satisfied with my good fortune. In the palace was a picture of a certain fairy named Svarnarekhâ, and my newly-married wife said to me privately one day: 'I must warn you, my husband, not to touch that picture of Svarnarekhâ.' For some time I refrained, but at last curiosity got the better of prudence, and I touched Svarnarekhâ with my hand. The fairy immediately stretched out her foot, and gave me such a vigorous kick, that I found myself back again in my own country. Since that day I have been a wanderer, and in the course of my roaming I reached this city, and went to lodge at the house of a cowherd. When I was living there, the cowherd, coming home one evening from the care of his herd, surprised his wife in conversation with a procuress, the wife of a barber. He therefore gave his wife a beating, and having tied her up to a post, went to sleep. In the middle of the night the confidante came back and said to the cowherd's wife: 'Your lover is almost expiring of love for you; do you go to him, and I meanwhile will tie myself up here.' They did as the confidante proposed, and soon after the cowherd woke up. He called out, 'Why don't you go to your lover?' The woman made no reply. The cowherd exclaimed in a rage, 'I suppose you are too proud to answer,' and having cut off her nose, went back again to sleep. Soon after this the cowherd's wife came back. 'What is the news?' she asked. 'News enough,' returned the confidante, 'as my face will show.' So the cowherd's wife loosed the confidante, tying herself up again, while the unfortunate woman, picking up her nose, went home. Next morning the barber asked his wife to give him the case of razors, when she, instead of giving him the box, took out one and gave it him. The barber said angrily, 'What do you mean by that?' and threw the razor from him. His wife—the confidante—immediately put her hands to her face as if in pain, and cried out: 'You have cut my nose off, and all for nothing!' and carried her complaint to the judge.

The cowherd meanwhile had narrowly questioned his wife as to the events of the preceding night. She, resenting the insinuation, exclaimed, 'You wicked wretch! who can bring any charge against me? Who can do me an injury? My conduct is blameless.

110 Sun and moon, wind and fire, heaven and earth, the heart and Yama, day and night, the morning and the evening twilight, and justice know the conduct of man.

If I then am virtuous, if I have not forsaken my husband, let my face be uninjured.' The cowherd then got a light, and seeing that his wife's face was uninjured, confessed himself in the wrong and apologized for his conduct. Such is the story of Svarnarekhâ and the confidante. "Now," continued Kandarpaketu, "look at this good man, the merchant, who is standing by. You shall hear his story. He went away from home, and after having travelled in the Malaya mountains for twelve years reached this city, where he found a lodging in the house of a lady of the town. Over her door was the figure of a demon, and in it was a very valuable jewel. The merchant, seeing this jewel, made up his mind to get possession of it, so with that intention he got up in the middle of night. No sooner had he touched it, than the demon laid hold of him, and gave him such a squeeze that he was forced to cry out. This woke up the mistress of the house, who got up and found the merchant in the grasp of the demon. 'Oh! my good sir!' she said, 'I understand you come from the Malaya mountains, so I have no doubt you have plenty of jewels. Unless you give them up you will not be let go. That is the way of this demon.' So the merchant had to give up all his jewels to get away from the image, and in this condition, having lost all his property, he has joined us."

"The officers of justice then," continued Damanaka, "having heard the story, punished them all round as they deserved: the barber's wife had her head shaved—the confidante had to pay a fine—the cowherd's wife was punished—but the merchant got back his property. We are in the same condition that they were: our misfortunes are all our own fault; therefore it would be absurd of us to complain. However," he suddenly exclaimed, "as I made the friendship between our master and the bull, I will find some means for putting an end to it; for:

111 Clever men can make untruths look like truths. Clever painters can make risings and hollows appear on an even surface.

112 He who does not lose his head when unexpected events occur, will get over diffi-

culties as the farmer's wife did her two lovers."

"How did that happen?" said Karataka.

Damanaka said:

STORY VII

In the town of Dvârâvatî, there lived a farmer whose wife was a person of very loose character. In the same town was a judge, and to this judge, as well as to his son, she used to pay special attention. For as has been said:

113 Wood will never satisfy a fire: rivers will never fill the ocean: death is never satiated with living creatures: nor will handsome women ever be tired of the attentions of men.

One day the judge's son came to pay her a visit, and soon after the judge himself was seen coming up to the house. So she shut up the son in a closet, and received the father with the same civility that she had shown to the son. Meanwhile her husband, the farmer, came home from his work in the fields. As soon as his wife saw him coming, she said to the judge, "Take up your stick and go away in a hurry, as if you were angry," which he did without hesitation. The farmer saw the judge leaving the house, and said: "What has the judge been doing here?" She replied, "He is angry with his son for some reason or other—I know not why—and the son came here and I hid him in the closet. His father followed him, and not finding him has gone off in a rage." So saying she produced the young man from the closet. Therefore

I say: He who does not lose his head when unexpected events occur will get over his difficulties like the farmer's wife.

"True enough," said Karataka, "but the friendship that exists between our master and Sanjîvaka is so firmly rooted, that I think it will not be broken without difficulty."

Damanaka replied, "Well, we must find some means or other; for as it has been said:

114 What cannot be done by force can often be done by stratagem. A crow caused a serpent to be put to death all through a golden chain."

"How came that about?" said Karataka.

Damanaka replied:

STORY VIII

A certain tree was the dwelling-place of a pair of crows. In its trunk lived a black serpent, which continually devoured the young crows. At length the female crow said to her mate: "My dear husband, I think we had better leave this tree for some other; as long as we remain here in the neighbourhood of the serpent, our children will never have any chance of growing up; for it has been said:

115 An ill-tempered wife—a false friend—an impudent servant—and dwelling in a house infested by serpents: these things are certain death."

"My dear," replied the Crow, "do not put yourself out; times without number we have suffered this injury, but now it can be endured no longer." "But how," returned his wife, "are you going to put a stop to the evils wrought by this terrible black serpent?" The Crow replied, "Don't trouble yourself about that; for:

116 The man who has knowledge, has strength:
But how can there be strength to a fool?

See how a lion in the pride of his power was overthrown by a rabbit."

The female Crow said, "And how was that?"

Her husband related the following story:

STORY IX

On a mountain called Mandara lived a lion who used to kill and eat the beasts who inhabited the same mountain. They therefore held a meeting, and passed a resolution that, to avoid the wholesale destruction that was going on, they would themselves voluntarily furnish each day an animal for the lion's meal. This was communicated to the Lion, who assented to this plan, and confined himself afterwards to the beast daily allotted him. It so happened that it came one day to an old rabbit's turn to be handed over, and he thought to himself:

117 "Great reverence is paid to this lion, through the hope of escaping destruction: if I must be killed and eaten, I must, but I certainly don't mean to be over and above respectful; so I shall not hurry myself about going."

The Lion was very hungry, and called out to the Rabbit in an angry tone of voice, "Why have you been so long coming?" The Rabbit replied, "I am very sorry, but it is not my fault: I was on the road, and another lion detained me. Before he let me go, he made me swear an oath to return, and I have come to tell your lordship this." The Lion was furious, and he exclaimed, "Where is this impudent scoundrel? Pray show me." The Rabbit answered, "If your lordship will follow me I will bring you to him"; and led him to a deep well full of clear transparent water. The Rabbit said, "This is where he dwells." The Lion looked in and saw his own reflection in the water. Bursting with rage and pride, he leaped down to make an attack on his supposed enemy, and was drowned. Therefore I say: The man who has knowledge has strength, but how can there be strength to a fool?

"Well," said the hen Crow, "I have heard your story; now pray tell me what you mean to do?" Her mate replied, "Every day the king's son comes and bathes in the pond close by: he always takes off the gold chain which he wears and places it on a flat-stone: you must take the chain off the stone while he is in the water, and put it into the hollow of the tree where the black serpent lives." Soon after this the prince came to bathe, and placed the gold chain on the stone as usual, when the Crow seized it and carried it into the hollow of the tree. The servants came to look for the chain, and in the course of the search they found the black serpent, and killed him. Wherefore I say, concluded Damanaka, What cannot be done by force can often be done by stratagem.

"If that be so," returned Karataka, "go to our master, and good luck go with you."

Damanaka then respectfully approached Pingalaka, and said: "Sir! I have been thinking over a matter which gives me some uneasiness, and I have come to tell you; for:

118 When disasters are at hand, when there is danger on a journey of losing the road, and when time and opportunity are slipping away—then an honest man, though unasked, should give good advice.

119 The Sovereign is a vessel of pleasure, but the Minister is a vessel of business. When the King's affairs go wrong, the Minister has to bear the blame.

The course marked out is clear:

120 It is better for a minister to sacrifice his life, or to lose his head, than to connive at the crime of one who aims at usurping his lord's place.

"Well," said Pingalaka kindly, "what is it that you have come to tell me?" Damanaka replied: "The truth is that Sanjîvaka has not been acting quite loyally towards your Majesty. Even in my presence he has spoken of you with disrespect, and seems to have an eye to the sovereignty."

Pingalaka, hearing this, felt considerably upset, and was silent for a time. Damanaka continued: "My lord, you must remember that you yourself got rid of your old servants and appointed this

Sanjîvaka to look after all your affairs. Now this was a great mistake ; for :

121 Fortune stands firmly on her feet supporting both the king and his minister in prosperity. But she cannot bear the burden of both because she is a woman, and she therefore eventually forsakes one of the two.

122 When a king makes his minister the sole ruler of the kingdom, the servant becomes infatuated through pride : then through sloth springing from pride he is ruined ; then a lust after sole power seizes on him, and under the influence of these passions his desire for independence leads him to compass the death of his prince.

123 Poisonous herbs, a loose tooth, an evil minister —these should be torn up by the roots if a man would have ease.

124 A king who makes his fortune dependent on a minister, will go to ruin when misfortune comes upon him, like a blind man without a guide.

A minister in this position acts according to his own will and pleasure. Here in this kingdom the sole authority is your Majesty : but this I know, having learnt it from experience ; that :

125 There is not a single man in the world who does not desire fortune : who does not look with longing eyes on the young and beautiful wife of his neighbour."

"Well," said the Lion, after some reflection, "this may all be true, but surely you must know that I have a great affection for Sanjîvaka.

126 A loved friend may have his faults, but he is none the less beloved for that: the body is subject to many disorders, but who does not love it?

127 A friend may do many things which are not right, but he still remains a friend: the fire may burn down a palace, but it will not forfeit our veneration."

"Sir," replied Damanaka, "that argument is faulty:

128 Fortune delights to follow the man—be he son, minister, or stranger—whom the king delights to honour.

129 The safe course, though it be unpleasant, brings peace in the end. Good fortune will always follow the man who speaks, or the man who listens to counsels of safety.

Your Majesty has turned away all your old servants, and put this stranger before them: this was not well done; for:

130 A sovereign should never patronize a stranger, for the faults of the old servants of his family. Nothing tends to the overthrow of a kingdom more than policy of that kind."

"All that you say," exclaimed the Lion, "seems to me incredible! Here is Sanjîvaka, who has been promoted by me to a place of high honour, and do you mean to say that he is plotting treason against me?" "Sir," replied Damanaka:

131 An evil disposed man will always follow his nature, however much he may be honoured, just as a dog's tail, do what you will to it, always remains curled.

132 The tail of a mongrel cur may be oiled, pressed, and tied up in bandages for twelve years; but as soon as it is unbound, it will go back to its natural state.

133 How can the affection of the wicked be gained by honours and liberality? A poison tree, though watered with amrit, will not bear wholesome fruit.

134 When a man sees another's ruin impending, he should always speak, though he be not asked. Good men know this to be their duty—the evil think quite differently.

If therefore your Majesty be injured by the treasonable malice of Sanjîvaha, I at least am clear from all blame, since I have given you warning."

Pingalaka reflected in silence:

135 On information given by another person punishment should not be inflicted. The king should investigate the matter himself, and reward or punish accordingly.

136 For a king to punish or to reward without having duly considered the merit or fault in each case, is to bring destruction on himself, as though he put his hand into the mouth of a poisonous serpent.

Pingalaka then turned to Damanaka and said: "Would it be well to reprove Sanjîvaka?" "Certainly not, your Majesty," replied Damanaka hastily, "that would be to break up our secret confidences; and it has been said:

137 Secret confidence is like the seed of a plant:

if it be broken, even but a little, it will not spring forth ; and again :

138 Whether it be in giving or in receiving, or in carrying out some work : delay in every case leads to failure.

Again : a matter once begun should be brought to completion with the utmost dispatch ; for :

139 Secret counsels are like a timid warrior : though fully armed, he cannot hold out long for fear of the enemy.

Though Sanjîvaka may possibly confess and repent of his evil doings, it would be very impolitic to renew friendship with him ; for :

140 He who admits to his counsels again a friend who has once deceived him, goes half-way to meet ruin and death."

"At any rate," said the Lion, "we ought clearly to understand what power Sanjîvaka has to damage us."

"Sir," answered Damanaka, "as long as it is not known what supporters a man has, how can there be any real knowledge of his power? The sea was overcome by a mere sandpiper."

"Pray how did that come about?" said the Lion.

Damanaka related the following story :

STORY X

A pair of sandpipers had made their nest on the seashore. The hen bird was just about to lay, and she said to her mate : "Cannot you find me some place convenient for laying my eggs?" "And is not this," he replied, "a very good place for the purpose?" "No," she answered, "for it is continually overflowed by the tide." "Am I, then, become so feeble," he exclaimed, "that the eggs laid in my house are to be carried away by the sea?" The hen sandpiper laughed and said: "There is some considerable difference between you and the sea."

Now it has been said:

141 He who has wisdom enough to know whether he is able to save himself out of a difficulty, need never sink under it.

142 To undertake an improper business: to quarrel with one's own family: to contend with one stronger than oneself: to put confidence in women: these are the four gates of death.

So at the bidding of her mate the hen sandpiper laid her eggs on the shore. The sea, who had overheard this conversation, was minded to try his strength, and carried off all the eggs. The hen bird was filled with lamentations, and exclaimed: "O, what a terrible disaster! my eggs are all gone!" "Never mind, my dear," replied her lord, "I will see what can be done"; and he forthwith calling the birds together, they all went in a body to Garuḍa, the king of the birds, and laid their complaint before him. Garuḍa heard what they had to say, and appealed to his lord the Divine Nârâyana—the creator, upholder, and destroyer of the universe. Nârâyana issued his orders to the sea, and Garuḍa returned with them on his crest. So the sea, on receiving the deity's commands, gave up the eggs; therefore I say: As long as it is not known what supporters a man has, how can there be any real knowledge of his power?

"But granting this," said the king, "how are we to know that he is ill-disposed to us?" "Easily," answered Damanaka. "When he comes before you as if he anticipated danger, prepared to rush at you with his horns down, then your Majesty will know very well." So saying, Damanaka went off to interview Sanjîvaka. He approached the bull very slowly, pretending to be overcome by fear and anxiety. Sanjîvaka addressed him with great kindness: "My dear Damanaka! I trust you are well and thriving?" "How is it possible," answered Damanaka, "for a servant to be well and thriving?

143 Their fate is in the power of another: their minds are full of anxiety: their very lives are not safe: such is the fate of those who put their trust in princes."

"My dear friend," returned Sanjîvaka, "what does this all mean?" "What answer can such a wretch as I give?" replied Damanaka.

144 "Just as a man who has fallen into the sea, and lays hold of a serpent, cannot hold on, and dare not let go: such is my miserable condition.

145 On the one hand, I must lose the confidence of my king: on the other, the love of my friend! Where can I go, what can I do, fallen into such an ocean of woe?"

Damanaka sighed deeply, and sat down in silence. "Still, my friend," said Sanjîvaka, "tell me exactly what you have on your mind." Damanaka took him aside and said: "It is not lawful for me to reveal the secret counsel of the king to another; but as you came here by my introduction, and I feel responsible for your safety, I will tell you what I think you ought to know. Our master has taken a dislike to you, and he has said confidentially to one of his friends, 'I am going to kill Sanjîvaka and feast my household on him.'" Sanjîvaka on hearing this was filled with consternation. Damanaka, however, bid him cheer up and look about, and see what was best to be done at this crisis. Sanjîvaka was quite at his wits' end, and could only muse on the hardness of his lot.

"How true it is," he exclaimed:

146 "Women are attracted by scoundrels: kings generally favour the undeserving: wealth is the portion of the miser: heaven sends its rain on the barren hills.

147 Lakshmî honours the worthless: Sarasvatî the man of low family: women enjoy the society of the blackguard: the cloud pours its waters on the mountain."

Sanjîvaka paused, and said to himself: Is this all the Jackal's doing or not? From his manner and appearance it is impossible to say; for:

148 An evil man often gains lustre from the excellence of his patron: he is like the black powder which women place round their eyes.

"What is the meaning of this disaster which has befallen me?" exclaimed Sanjîvaka.

149 "A king may be dissatisfied, though he be served with the utmost care. That is not to be wondered at. But here is one who becomes a most deadly enemy, though I have devoted myself to him.

This my unremitting diligence then is useless; for:

150 He who is angry for any reason, may be pacified if the reason is removed; but when a man's mind is hostile without any reason, how is he to be won over?

What offence have I committed against the king?" continued Sanjîvaka; "or do kings become hostile without any cause for anger?" "It is so," replied Damanaka.

151 A hundred kind acts are thrown away on the evil:
A hundred wise sayings on the stupid:
A hundred warnings on those who will not take advice:
A hundred pieces of advice on the thoughtless.

152 Serpents hide in the sandal trees: alligators lurk among the lotuses in the rivers: envious men spy out all our enjoyments: there is no pleasure that we can enjoy unhindered.

153 The root is infested by snakes: the flowers are full of bees: the branches of monkeys: the top by bears. What part of the sandal tree is not full of the vilest impurities?

"Our master," continued Damanaka, "has honey on his tongue and poison in his heart: I know him well.

154 There is a man whose hand is stretched out to greet us—whose eyes are moist with affection—who offers us a seat beside himself—who embraces us with affection—who is full of kind inquiries—who is honey outside, but has poison concealed within his heart—a man of guile. Ah! what a wonderful art of dissimulation is that which the wicked have learned!

155 A ship has been devised for crossing the ocean—a lamp for lighting up the darkness—a fan for cooling the heat: a hook to restrain an elephant mad with passion. There is nothing on earth for which some expedient has not been found by the Creator; but even the Creator himself could not turn aside the thoughts of the wicked."

"But what an injustice," returned Sanjîvaka, "that I, who live on herbs, should be killed by the Lion! for:

156 Between two of equal strength: between two of equal position: a quarrel may be imagined: but not between two persons one of whom is highly exalted, the other very humble.

By whom, I wonder," he thought, "has our master been turned against me? A king who is determined to act as an enemy must always be a subject of alarm; for:

157 If the mind of a king, as delicate as a crystal bracelet, be perverted by his advisers, who can restore it whole again?

158 Two things are very terrible: a thunderbolt

and the wrath of a sovereign : but one falls on only one place, the other everywhere.

Death, then, must be faced in the contest : for it is unfitting to obey his commands.

159 A valiant man either dies in the fight and gains paradise, or kills his enemy and gains peace : both of these blessings are very difficult to gain—to be gained only by a valiant man.

There is a time too for the fight ; for :

160 When without fighting destruction is certain, and with fighting there is a possibility of life, wise men call that the time for battle.

161 When there is nothing left in life to desire ; then a wise man dies fighting with his enemy.

162 By victory he may gain fortune : by death a heavenly consort : bodies perish in a moment ; why should there be any hesitation to die in battle ?"

All these thoughts passed through the mind of Sanjîvaka, and he turned to Damanaka and said : "My dear friend, how may I know that the Lion means to kill me ? What signs will he show of his intention ?" Damanaka replied, "When he pricks up his ears, lashes his tail, lifts up his paw, glares at you with his mouth wide open—then you may be quite sure he means to kill you, and you must put on a bold front ; for :

163 A man may be strong, but if he is cowardly he is an object of contempt. No one is afraid of treading on an heap of ashes.

All this conversation of ours, however," continued Damanaka, "must be kept in the dark; otherwise what the consequence to us would be I am sure I don't know."

Damanaka having finished his task, went back to Karataka. "Well," said Karataka, "and how have you got on with the Lion and Sanjîvaka?" "I think," replied he, "that I have contrived to set them both by the ears." "It is just as I anticipated," answered Karataka; for:

164 Who would be a friend to the wicked? who would not be angry if he were always being importuned? Who could not be corrupted by riches? Who could not become skilled in evil?

165 To gain their own ends scoundrels will corrupt a virtuous man: will not intercourse with the wicked destroy like a fire?"

Damanaka then went to Pingalaka. "Sir!" said he, "the ill-conditioned traitor is just on the point of coming," and made the Lion assume the attitude which was to be the sign of his hostility. Sanjîvaka soon after appeared, and seeing the aggressive appearance of the Lion, for which he had been prepared by Damanaka, responded by a corresponding show of defiance. A terrific combat then ensued, the end of which was that Sanjîvaka was killed by the Lion. No sooner had this been done, than Pingalaka repented and exclaimed, "What an abominable crime is this that I have committed; for here:

166 The sovereign is a vessel of iniquity, while

others enjoy his kingdom. This is an outrage on justice, and a king who acts thus is as a lion who kills an elephant.

167 There is a difference between the loss of a piece of territory and of a wise and good minister. The loss of the minister is the destruction of the prince ; the lost territory may be recovered."

"Your Majesty," said Damanaka, "what is the meaning of all this argument to show that remorse should be felt for the slaughter of an enemy? Has it not been said :

168 If a father, or a brother, or a son, or a friend, seek the king's life, they must be put to death by the prince if he wishes to keep possession of his power.

169 A king who truly understands his duty, his advantage, and his pleasure, should not be extremely compassionate : for he who is over lenient cannot keep his dominions, although they be under his rule.

170 Truly the forgiveness of friends and foes is the virtue which adorns the religious : it is a fault in a king to extend his forgiveness to those who have committed crimes.

171 When a servant through pride or desire of sovereignty aims at his lord's kingdom, there is no expiation possible except death.

172 An over-merciful king : a Brâhman who eats all things : a disobedient wife : an unruly servant : a cross-grained friend : a careless superintendent : and a man who does not

acknowledge a kindness: these are persons to be avoided.

173 The policy of princes must be ever changing: by turns true and false; rough and smooth; cruel and merciful; miserly and liberal: always spending, yet always heaping up money."

The heart of Pingalaka gradually attained a state of tranquillity. Soothed by the skilful arguments of Damanaka, he recovered his spirits, and once more took his seat on the throne. Damanaka was overjoyed at the result of his manœuvres, and approaching the king with a low obeisance said: "May your Majesty ever be victorious over your enemies, and may perfect happiness be your portion." With these words Damanaka sat down at his ease, perfectly satisfied with himself.

"Such," said Vishṇuśarman to the Princes, "is the 'Separation of Friends.'"

The Princes answered, "We have been indeed gratified."

"Before we conclude," continued Vishṇuśarman, "this must be added:

174 May quarrels between friends exist only in the abodes of your enemies.

May traitors, as the days go by, approach their destruction nearer and nearer.

May happiness and prosperity ever dwell among the men of our land;

And may boys of after time rejoice in the garden of fable."

III

VIGRAHA

WAR

VIGRAHA

WAR

"SIR!" said the Princes on another occasion, when Vishṇuśarman was continuing his instruction, "we are the sons of a king, and we should like to hear something about war." "By all means," replied Vishṇuśarman," "if that be your wish, I will tell your Highnesses what I have to say about war, and I propose as the foundation of our subject the following verse :

1 When there was war between the Geese and the Peacocks, the Geese, confiding in the Crows who lived in the dwellings of the enemy, were betrayed by them."

"And how was that?" said the Princes.

Vishṇuśarman proceeded to relate the following :

STORY I

There is a lake called Padmakelî in Karpûradvîpa, and in it there dwelt a Flamingo whose name was Hiraṇyagarbha, who had been made king by the birds of the lake in solemn assembly ; for :

2 If there were not a king able to lead the people, they would be tossed about like a ship at sea without a rudder.

3 The king guards the people: the people enrich the king. Protection is more than riches. Where there is no protector that which exists does not exist.

The Flamingo was sitting one day on a bed of lotuses, with his attendants round him, when a Crane, called Dîrghamukha, who had arrived from a long journey, came up, and having saluted his sovereign, sat down. "Dîrghamukha," exclaimed the King, "you have come from a far country: tell us, what is the news?" "Sir," answered Dîrghamukha, "there is great news, and I have made haste to come and tell your Majesty. There is a mountain in Jambudvîpa called Vindhya: a Peacock, whose name is Chitravarṇa, lives there, and he is king of the birds. I was walking about one day in the middle of a wood, when I met some of his attendants. They came up to me and asked me my name and country. I replied that I came from Karpûradvîpa, and that I was one of King Hiraṇyagarbha's attendants, and added that I was travelling in a foreign country out of curiosity. When the birds heard this they said: 'Well, of the two, which country and king is the best?' 'What a question!' said I. 'There is an enormous difference between this country and our own: first of all, Karpûradvîpa is paradise: and its king is equal to the lord of Paradise: indeed, it passes description. I wonder how you can stay in such a wretched place as this, you had much better come and live in the country I come from.' When the birds heard this they grew very angry; as it is said:

4 As a draught of milk given to serpents only increases their venom, so advice given to fools only aggravates their folly.

5 A man of sense may profit by advice, but never a fool: the birds which gave good advice to some ignorant monkeys were, as a consequence, driven out of their homes.

"How did that come about?" said Chitravarṇa.

Dîrghamukha related the following:

STORY II

On the banks of the Narmadâ there is a large Sâlmalî tree, growing in a valley, in which some birds had built their nests and lived there even during the rains. Now the rainy season had set in, the sky was as black as pitch, and presently there was a heavy storm. The birds looked out of their nests and saw the monkeys shivering in the cold and wet, at the foot of the tree. They called out to them and said:

6 "We have built our nests with straw which we have got together, and we only have bills: You have hands and feet, and yet you sit there homeless and in despair. How is this?"

The monkeys, hearing these remarks, grew very angry. They said, "Just listen! Here are these birds warm and comfortable in their nests, laughing at us. Just wait till the rain stops, and then see what will happen." And so it was, that when the storm cleared, the monkeys climbed the tree, tore down the nests and broke all the eggs. Therefore I say: A man with sense may profit by good advice, but never a fool.

"Well," said the Flamingo, "what did the birds do then?"

The birds, replied Dîrghamukha, grew furious and said: "Pray who made the Flamingo king?" "Pray who made the Peacock king?" I retorted. When the birds heard this they were ready to kill me, so I put the boldest face on the matter that I could.

7 Patience is an ornament to a man, modesty to a woman: but there are times when these virtues are becoming to neither."

The King laughed and said:

8 "He who comparing his own strength and weakness with that of his enemies does not recognize the difference between them, will be overthrown.

9 The stupid ass who wandered about the fields in a lion's skin, eating the corn, was at last found out by his voice and killed."

The Crane said: "How was that?"

The Flamingo said:

STORY III

In Hastinâpura there was a washerman named Vilâsa, whose ass by a course of hard work and low feeding had been brought to the verge of extinction. So the washerman dressed him up in a tiger's skin and turned him out to graze in a field of corn. The owner of the field came up, and seeing the animal, ran away, thinking it was a tiger. A man, however, who had been watching the field, had his suspicions, wrapped himself up in a grey blanket, and taking his bows and arrows, went on all fours into the field. The ass, whose vigour had been restored by rest and food, saw him, and thinking that it was another ass, trotted up to him and set up a loud braying. This revealed the secret of his identity, and he was immediately killed by the owners of the field. Therefore I say: He who comparing his own strength and weakness with that of his enemies does not recognize the difference between them, will be overthrown.

When the King had finished his story Dîrghamukha continued: The birds became infuriated and shouted, "You scoundrelly Crane! How dare you, an alien, revile our sovereign. This is past endurance." And they rushed at me and struck me with their beaks, exclaiming, "You are a blockhead, your king after all is only a gander; he isn't fit to be a king: how can a miserable gander keep order and rule: what sort of a kingdom can he have? You know no more of the world than a frog in a well, and that is why you think so much of your king and country; for it has been said:

10 A great tree is to be desired for its fruit and its shade, but if there be no fruit, why should not its shade be made the most of?

11 No respect should be paid to low persons: the great alone are to be held in reverence. Even water in the hands of a tavern keeper is called wine. Besides:

12 Even a mighty man, possessed of all the virtues, may lose his position, if he has weak or worthless supporters: he is as an elephant seen in a mirror.

13 By stratagem a very powerful king may be worsted. By a stratagem, in which the Moon had a part, the Rabbits managed to live in peace."

"What is the meaning of that?" I asked.

The Birds said:

STORY IV

One summer some elephants were very much distressed by the heat, and said to their leader: "We are absolutely perishing for want of water. The smaller animals have bathing places, but we have none, and we are, as it were, blinded. What are we to do? Where are we to go?"

The leader of the herd, having made some investigations, found a pond for them to bathe in. This pond was however already frequented by rabbits, and the rabbits were trampled down by the elephants when they came to bathe, so that numbers of them were killed. One of them named Silîmukha was very unhappy at this, and thought to himself: "If this sort of thing goes on, there will soon not be a rabbit left." A cunning old buck called Vijaya, guessing the cause of his dejected appearance, said: "Cheer up! I will find some remedy or other." With this Vijaya started off, and on the way set to work to consider what would be the best way to approach these elephants; for it is said:

14 The touch of an elephant: the kiss of a serpent: the patronage of a king: the smile of a traitor. There is death in all these.

So he thought to himself, "I will go to the top of the hill and address myself to the Elephant King." When the King saw him coming he said: "Pray who are you, and what do you want?" The Rabbit said, "I am an ambassador from his majesty Chandra—the Moon." The Elephant King replied: "Declare your errand." Vijaya replied:

15 "Even after the weapons of war have been unsheathed an ambassador speaks not otherwise than he has been commanded. According to his sacred character he ever says only that which is true."

"By my lord's commands, I speak: I am Saśânka. That is my name, for I bear the rabbit on my face. Now you have driven away the rabbits who are the guardians of my pool. Therefore you have committed a great crime."

When the Elephant heard this he was terrified, and said: "Sir! I have sinned through ignorance: I will do so no more!" The Ambassador replied: "Well, then! if you will come and worship Chandra, who is in the pond, quivering with rage, you may go in peace." The Elephant gladly assented, and Vijaya led him to the pond by night, where he saw the moon's reflection in the ripples on the pond. He made a humble obeisance and said: "Mighty deity! I ask pardon for my fault. I have sinned through ignorance; I will do so no more."

After this expression of penitence the lord of

the elephants was dismissed by Vijaya, and the rabbits ever after enjoyed their pond in peace and quiet. Therefore we say: By a stratagem a very powerful king may be worsted.

When the birds had finished I said: "Our Sovereign is great in dignity and power: he is worthy to rule the three worlds: how much more a single kingdom." The birds then conducted me to the presence of their king, Chitravarṇa, after having lavished a considerable amount of abuse on me. "May it please your Majesty," said the birds bringing me into the royal presence, "here is an abominable Crane, who not only trespasses on our land, but speaks with disrespect of you." "Who is he, and where does he come from?" said the King. "He is a subject of the Flamingo Hiraṇyagarbha," they answered, "and he comes from Karpûradvîpa." The Prime Minister, who was a Vulture, then said to me: "Who is their Prime Minister, then?" I replied, "A Chakravâka named Sarvajna. He is a learned person, skilled in every science." "It is well," answered the Vulture, "he is a fitting prime minister; for:

16 It is fitting that a king should appoint as his minister a native of the land, performing the duties of his caste without fault, of unblemished loyalty, skilled in all the sciences, free from vice, not given to loose pleasures, learned in the law, famous, of noble family, intelligent, able to manage the finances of the kingdom with profit."

A Parrot then rose up and said, "Sir! If I remember rightly, this Karpûradvîpa and the other islands, are an outlying portion of your Majesty's own dominions. Your authority extends over them." "Quite true: it is so," answered the King; for:

17 Kings, madmen, children, women, and those who are proud of their money may desire what cannot be attained: how much more reasonably what can."

I replied, "If mere assertion is to give your Majesty a right over Karpûradvîpa, the same authority will give my sovereign Hiraṇyagarbha a right over Jambudvîpa." "How are you going to prove that?" said the Parrot. "By war," I replied. "Well, then," said King Chitravarṇa, with a smile, "go back to your lord and make preparation for war." "Will not your Majesty send your own ambassador with this challenge?" I asked. "Certainly," replied the King turning to his attendants; "which of you is ready to go? for an ambassador must be appointed:

18 An ambassador should be a Brâhman, prompt, knowing the secrets of another's heart, loyal, accomplished, adroit, resolute, free from vice, patient."

The Vulture said, "There are many possessed of these qualities; but still on such a mission as this a Brâhman should be sent; for:

19 It is a gracious manner in an envoy which gains the king what he desires, not exalted birth: even 'Siva himself cannot get rid of the black poison which stains his neck."

The King said: "Very well! the Parrot shall go?" and turning to the Parrot he said: "Go along with the Crane and bear our message to Hiraṇyagarbha." "As your Majesty commands," answered the Parrot; "but this Crane is an evil disposed person; I will not travel in company with villains like him; for it has been said:

20 A villain will carry corruption with him, he will even infect the virtuous. The ten-headed Râvana was able to carry off Sîta: even the ocean may be held in bondage.

21 I will not stay, nor will I go with a villain. A Gander was standing with a Crow—a Quail was travelling along with a Crow; both alike came to destruction."

"How was that?" said the King.

The Parrot answered:

STORY V

On side of the road leading to Ujjayinî stands a large pippal tree, and in it a Gander and a Crow had made their dwelling together. One hot season a certain Traveller, tired out with the heat, laid down under the tree, and putting his bow and arrows by his side, went to sleep. Presently as the day went on, the shade of the tree ceased to fall on the Traveller, and his face became exposed to the rays of the sun. The Gander observed this, and being a bird of kindly, charitable disposition, stretched out his wings and shaded the Traveller's face from the glare. The Traveller was lying on his back fast asleep, with his mouth wide open, when the ill-natured Crow, who could not bear to see another enjoying himself, took careful aim and let his droppings fall into the sleeper's mouth. The Crow then flew away, and the Traveller, suddenly waking up, saw the Gander perching on the tree above him. So he hastily seized his bow and arrows and instantly shot the Gander dead. Therefore I say: I will not stay, nor will I go with a villain.

22 Avoid the companionship of the wicked, follow after the virtuous: do good day and night, recollecting that all things pass away.

"Sir," continued the Parrot, "such is the story of the Gander who lived with a Crow. Now I will relate to you the story of the Quail who travelled with a Crow."

STORY VI

A certain Crow lived in the branch of a tree, and below him on the ground dwelt a Quail. One day the birds all went on a pilgrimage to the sea-shore in honour of Garuḍa, and the Quail walked in company with his friend the Crow. On the road they saw a cowherd, who was carrying on his head a pot of curds, and the Crow kept on continually pecking at the curds and eating them. The herdsman at length put the pot on the ground, and looking up saw the Crow and the Quail. The Crow immediately flew away and escaped, but the Quail, being heavy and slow of motion, was caught and killed. Therefore I say again: I will not stay, nor will I go with a villain.

On hearing these stories I remonstrated with the Parrot, and asked him why he imputed such evil intentions to me. I said to him: "My respect for you is as great as it is for the King himself." "Possibly," replied the Parrot, "but:

23 The words of a villain may be soft and accompanied by smiles, but they are like flowers out of season,—I am afraid of them. Besides, your wickedness is evident from your words, for if war should break out between the two kings it is your words that have been the cause of it.

24 It is easy enough to conciliate a blockhead, even though the offence be committed under his own eyes. A wheelwright once placed his own wife and her lover on his head."

"Pray how did that come about?" said the King. The Parrot related the following:

STORY VII

There was a wheelwright called Mandamati who lived in 'Srînagara. He knew that his wife had a lover, but he had never been able to catch her. So one day, saying to his wife, "I am going on a journey to a distant town," he went a little way on the road and then came back, and without her knowing anything about it, returned home and hid under the bed. When his wife was quite sure (as she thought,) that he was well out of the way, she invited her lover to come and spend the evening with her. It so happened that while she was entertaining him, she accidentally discovered that her husband was hidden under the bed, and in consequence relaxed her hospitable attentions to her guest. He complained, "Why, how is this? You are quite chilly and stand-off to-day; what is the matter?" She replied with a melancholy air: "Well I may be! he who is everything to me is gone away, and I don't know when I shall see him again. Perhaps he may be homeless and starving: without him the world is a desert." "You don't mean to say," retorted her lover, "that you care so much for your disagreeable, quarrelsome husband?" "You are an unfeeling wretch," answered the wife; "what are you saying? Just listen to this:

25 The wife who, meeting with rough words or angry looks from her husband, always looks at him with a smiling countenance—she is truly a virtuous woman.

26 That woman is the inheritor of everlasting happiness who loves her husband, whether he be polite or rude, a saint or a sinner.

27 A husband is a woman's chief glory, she needs no other: deprived of him, though covered with ornaments she has no beauty.

You must recollect," she continued, "that after all you are only a lover; you are only to be made use of, like flowers, or betel nuts, or sandalwood, to gratify a fancy: but he, my lord, can sell me to the gods if he will, or give me to the Brâhmans. I cannot say more! While he lives I will live too. I will not survive him—this I am determined; for:

28 The wife who clings to her dead husband on

the funeral pile, and resigns her own life, shall enter the mansion of the gods, and take her husband with her, though he may have committed sins without number.

29 To whom her father, or her brother by her father's command, has given her, him while living she must obey, when dead she must follow."

The wheelwright, who was under the bed, heard all this, and he thought to himself, "Well! I am in luck; it is not every one who has got such an affectionate and dutiful wife as I have." And raising up the bed, with his wife and her lover sitting upon it, on his head, the great fool danced for joy. Therefore I say: It is easy enough to conciliate a blockhead, though the offence be committed under his own eyes.

When the Parrot had finished his story, the King bade me farewell. I immediately started on my return, and the Parrot is just behind me. So you must consider what is best to be done."

The Chakravâka, the Prime Minister, said with a sneer: "Sir! This Crane has performed your Majesty's business to the best of his ability: but he has acted like a fool; for:

30 Wise men say that it is better to make any compromise rather than to fight, but to fight without cause is the mark of a fool."

"It is of no use," replied the King, "to quarrel over what is past: the present emergencies must be provided for." "Certainly, your Majesty," replied the Chakravâka, "but I would speak with you on this matter in private; for:

31 Shrewd persons can interpret the thoughts by the colour, by the appearance, by sounds, by a change in the eye or the mouth—therefore we should take counsel in private.

So the King and his minister remained there, while the rest went away. The Chakravâka began: "Sir! I suspect that this business has been brought about by the Crane, at the suggestion of some of your Majesty's ministers; for:

32 The sick are the best subjects for physicians:
The vicious are the object of the king's officers:
Fools are a source of profit to the wise:
The discreet are the king's best friends."

"All this may be true enough," said the King; "but we can look into the cause of it all afterwards. Just consider what is the best thing to do now." "Sir!" answered the Chakravâka, "let us send a spy into that country and find out exactly what its strength and weakness is; for:

33 The business of a spy is to see what ought or ought not to be done, in his own country, and in foreign countries. He is the eye of the king: without spies the king is blind.

I therefore advise that a spy be sent, and that he should take with him a confidential assistant. When he has got together trustworthy information as to the condition and forces of the country, he should send home his assistant with the news, and remain there himself. For it has been said:

34 The king should correspond with his emis-

saries, and they should wear the badge of ascetics, who are supposed to be acquiring sacred knowledge at pilgrimages, shrines, and temples.

Besides this, a secret emissary ought to be able to travel either by water or land, so I should advise the appointment of the Crane to the office, associating with him another of his own kind, and that his follower should remain outside the palace of the king to whom they are sent. This must all be managed with the utmost secrecy; for:

35 Counsel in which six ears have a share, leaks out, and becomes public property: therefore the king should not take more than one person into his confidence.

36 Misfortunes which happen to a king through the revealing of counsel cannot be repaired: such is the opinion of those skilled in policy."

The King after reflecting for a moment said: "I think I have found an envoy in whom we can trust." "If that is so," answered the Chakravâka, "victory is certain."

Just at that moment they were interrupted by a chamberlain, who appeared, and said with a profound bow, "Your Majesty, a Parrot has arrived as an ambassador from Jambudvîpa, and he desires an audience of your Majesty." The King and the Chakravâka looked at one another for an instant, and then the Chakravâka said: "Let him be conducted to the apartment which has been prepared for him, and the presentation to your Majesty can be made in due form later." "As your Highness commands," replied the chamberlain, and he retired, with a view of conducting the Parrot to his abode. "So," said the King, "war is a certainty." "It appears so," replied the Chakravâka, "but we must proceed cautiously; for:

37 No prudent minister will, at the very outset of matters, and without due consideration, recommend his sovereign either to fight, or abdicate:

38 He will try to overcome his enemies, but not by war, if he can help it, for the result of a fight between two combatants is always doubtful. Besides:

39 By conciliation, by bribes, by sowing division—by these means either together or separately he will try to subvert his enemies, but not by force.

40 A man may be valiant enough who has never been in battle: and he who does not know his enemies' strength is very likely to despise them.

41 A rock is not raised so easily by the strength of man as by machinery: great results come from small means: such is the result of counsel.

But inasmuch as war is impending, let us proceed with vigour.

42 As cultivation of the land brings forth fruit by means of labour at the right season, so this policy will bring forth fruit; not immediately perhaps, but after a time.

43 Fear while the enemy is far off, but courage

when he is coming near, that is the character of a brave man. When misfortune approaches the man of courage acquires fortitude.

44 Haste is certainly the impediment in all cases to success. Does not water, however cold it may be, penetrate the earth by degrees?

Especially, your Majesty, it should be recollected that Chitravarṇa, the king of the peacocks, is very strong.

45 There is no law bidding us fight with one stronger than ourselves. A conflict with an elephant is not like an encounter with a man.

46 The man who would attack his enemy without waiting for the opportunity is a fool. A contest with the powerful is like trying to fly with an insect's wing.

47 Remaining in his tortoise-like shelter, a man of prudence should wait the attack, and then, when the time has come, he should rush out like an infuriated serpent.

Hear what I say, your Majesty:

48 Whether the foe be weak or powerful, the man of expedient will be equally ready: the river current can uproot the mighty tree just as easily as the grass.

Then let the Parrot be kept here, and entertained, until the fort has been got ready; for:

49 One bowman behind a rampart can stand against a hundred—a hundred against ten thousand, therefore I advise a fort.

50 A country without a fortress is liable to attack from an enemy. A king without a fortress is

like a man who has fallen overboard into the sea.

51 He should build a fortress with a great ditch and a lofty rampart on a high rock, having water and furnished with military engines, protected by a river, a desert, and a wood.

52 The seven things necessary in a fortress are spaciousness, difficulty of access, stores of liquor, grain, and fuel, with easy ingress and egress."

The King said: "Who should be employed to build and provision this fortress?" The Chakravâka answered:

53 "Whosoever is skilled, to him should your Majesty entrust the work; a man who has had no experience, though he be a learned man, would be of no use."

"Then," replied the King, "send for the Sârasa, the commander-in-chief of the army."

So the Sârasa was sent for, and when he arrived the King said: "Put the fortress into order without delay." The Sârasa bowed and replied: "Sir! the fortress has long been ready. We have a large pool, which will serve admirably, but let a store of corn be laid up on a stone in the middle of it; for:

54 May it please your Majesty, a store of grain is the best thing there is: a jewel put into the mouth would not keep a man alive; moreover:

55 Salt is the best seasoning that exists, for without that sauce has no savour."

"My worthy commander-in-chief," replied the King, "get together all the supplies you can possibly want without delay." Just at that moment a chamberlain entered, who said: "May it please your Majesty, the King of the Crows, whose name is Meghavarṇa, has just arrived from Jambudvîpa and desires an audience with your Majesty."

The King answered: "The crow is a bird of wisdom, and has seen much: therefore he ought to be honourably received." "This is true," said the Chakravâka; "still he is a land bird, and on the side of our enemies. How can we receive him with honour; for it has been said:

56 The fool who, deserting his own side, goes over to the enemy, courts his own destruction, like the blue jackal."

"Pray," said the King, "how was that?" The Chakravâka related the following:

STORY VIII

A jackal was once wandering about the suburbs of a town and fell into an indigo vat. He was unable to get out, and so when the owner of the indigo came in the morning, he lay still pretending to be dead. The man pulled him out, and taking him away some little distance, threw him down and left him. The jackal then got up and ran away into a wood. On looking himself over to see what damage he had received, he found that he was dyed a rich blue, and he thought to himself: "I ought to be able to make something out of my magnificent appearance." So he got together all the jackals, and he addressed them as follows: "Do you see my splendid colour? I have been anointed to the sovereignty of this wood by the goddess herself who rules over it, and this is the result. Nothing hereafter must be carried out in this forest except by my order." The jackals were much impressed by his appearance and colour, and professed absolute submission to his orders. After a time, however, he induced lions and tigers and other animals of a much superior order to accept his authority, and began to look down upon the jackals and to treat them with contempt. Indeed, he would have nothing whatever to say to his own immediate relations. An old jackal, who was wiser than the rest, perceiving their annoyance and vexation, said: "Don't be annoyed: I will undertake to put an end to this ill-conditioned stuck-up kinsman of ours. The tigers and these other beasts who have submitted to his rule don't know that he is only a jackal. Now do exactly as I tell you: when the evening comes you go close by him and set up a yelling; when he hears that he will respond, and make exactly the same noise; for:

57 There is not a single person who can conceal his natural character for long: if a dog were made king he would still try to gnaw the strap of your shoe.

When the tigers recognize the jackal by his voice they will set on him and kill him; for it has been said:

58 Our enemies soon find out our inmost strength

and weakness, and having found it out, will consume us, as a dry tree is burnt up by fire."

And so it came to pass as the jackal had said; therefore I say: The fool who, deserting his own side, goes over to the enemy, courts his own destruction.

"What you say," rejoined the King, "is doubtless true; still this Crow has come from some distance, and I think we ought to hear what he has to say."

"Please, your Majesty," answered the Chakravâka, "as the spy has been dispatched to Jambudvîpa, and the fortress is all ready, the Parrot might be interviewed and allowed to depart. But it must be recollected that:

59 Chanakya slew Nanda by means of a subtle envoy.

Therefore let the King be surrounded by his guards, and let the ambassador be interviewed at a respectful distance."

An assembly was therefore summoned, and the Parrot was conducted into King Hiraṇyagarbha's presence.

The Parrot entered with haughty mien, and delivered himself in the following manner: "Hiraṇyagarbha! The high and mighty King Chitravarṇa sends you these commands: If you desire to preserve your life and your kingdom, come and pay homage to us without delay, otherwise you had better go away to the uttermost ends of the earth."

Hiraṇyagarbha on hearing this was filled with wrath, and exclaimed: "Is there no one among these our followers who can silence this miscreant?" The Crow Meghavarṇa rose up and said: "Give me permission, your Majesty, and I will kill this impudent Parrot." "Not so, my worthy Meghavarṇa," interposed the Prime Minister; "listen to me:

60 That is no Council, where there are no elders: Those are not elders who do not speak according to law: that is not law, which is not after the truth: that is not truth, which is spoken under the influence of fear.

For the law is this:

61 An ambassador, though he be a savage, must not be put to death, for the king speaks through him. Though the weapons of war have been unsheathed, the ambassador cannot speak otherwise than he has been commanded.

62 Who, at the mere word of an envoy, would accept his own inferiority, or the superiority of another? An ambassador, because his person is inviolate, always delivers his whole message."

On hearing the good advice of the Chakravâka, the King and the Crow recovered their equanimity, and the Parrot, having performed the duty laid upon him, paid his respects and prepared to depart.

The Chakravâka, however, took him aside before leaving, and after apologizing for the rudeness to which he had been subjected, gave him suitable presents, bid him farewell, and started him on the road to his own country.

The Parrot journeyed along, and in course of time reached his home in the Vindhya mountains. He immediately went to report the result of his embassy to King Chitravarṇa, who was delighted to see him, and asked him what sort of a country Karpûradvîpa was. The Parrot replied: "An expedition should be immediately fitted out. Karpûradvîpa is a most desirable country; in fact, it is a perfect paradise, and should be brought under your Majesty's dominion without delay." The King called together his Council, and after putting the matter before them said: "My lords, we should be glad of your advice, for an invasion of Karpûradvîpa must be carried out immediately." The Prime Minister of Sambudvîpa, a Vulture named Dûradarśîn, got up and said: "Sir, all the circumstances under which we are going to enter upon this war should be carefully considered before we begin; for:

63 When friends, ministers, and allies are loyal and strong, and when those on the side of the enemy are quite the reverse—then is the time for war.

64 There are three results attainable by war—increase of territory, allies, and treasure; when those results are certain, then is the time for war."

"True," answered the King. "Meanwhile let the commander-in-chief review my forces, and let their number and efficiency be ascertained; and let the astrologers be summoned, so that they may appoint an auspicious time for starting on the campaign." "Your Majesty's orders shall be obeyed," answered the Prime Minister; for:

65 The fools who hastily plunge into a contest without finding out the enemy's strength, shall assuredly fall by the edge of the sword."

"Do not be ever throwing cold water on my energy," said the King, "but tell me the best way of making a successful incursion into the enemy's country; for I am perfectly determined on war, and on conquest too." "I will tell your Majesty," replied the Vulture, "the rules which should be followed, but if there is to be any satisfactory result, they must be very carefully attended to:

66 Advice given to a prince, even if founded on books which teach policy, is no use unless it be followed. The mere knowledge of the proper medicine will not cure a disease.

The commands of a sovereign," continued the Vulture, "must be obeyed; therefore I will tell you what I have learned:

The commander-in-chief must lead when a difficulty arises, accompanied by all the bravest men in the army; the women the prince, and the treasure must occupy the centre. The cavalry must be placed on the flanks, then the chariots and elephants; on the outside the infantry. The treasure should always accompany the king, and he should distribute it liberally among the fighting men. Man is not the slave of man, but of wealth. A horse is the strength of armies: the king who is superior in cavalry will gain the victory. The best force is that composed of brave men skilled in arms—enduring—made up chiefly of Kshâtriyas. A small army of valiant men is better than a large host of cowards, and the king should retain the affection of his soldiers. The king, after victory, should depopulate his enemy's country; for——"

"Well, after all," exclaimed the King, "breaking in upon his minister's harangue, "what is the need of so much talk? Surely:

67 Policy is success on one's own side, and defeat on the side of the enemy: admitting this, the policy taught by Vâchaspati must be carried out in action."

The Minister replied with a smile: "True; but:

68 The nature of one person is unrestrained, of another is amenable to law: light and darkness are not governed by the same law."

Before long the astrologers announced that a propitious day had arrived for the expedition, and King Chitravarṇa started at the head of his army. At the same time a messenger was sent to Karpûradvîpa by Hiraṇyagarbha's spy, to tell him that the invading army had actually started and was encamped at the foot of the Malaya mountain. The messenger added that it would be wise to retire to the fortress, for the Vulture, who was Prime Minister, was a very bold and skilful leader. Besides this, he said that there was someone in the fortress in the Vulture's pay, and that he had found this out from some stray expressions dropped by a confidant of the Minister. "This must be the Crow!" exclaimed the Chakravâka. "Impossible," returned the King, "for in that case

he would not have been so eager to kill the Parrot. Besides, King Chitravarṇa's determination to make war was not settled until after the Parrot's departure, and the Crow has been here a long while."
"It may be so," replied the Minister; "still, a foreigner must always be an object of suspicion."
"But even strangers," answered the King, "are capable of repaying kindnesses; for:

69 Even a stranger, if he be kindly disposed, is a friend; but a relation, if he be hostile, is an enemy. A disease may be bred in the body, but it is malignant: a medicine may come from the forest, but it tends to healing.

70 There was a servant to King 'Sûdraka, named Vîravara, who gave up his own son."

The Chakravâka said: "How did that happen?"

The King said:

STORY IX

I was once living in a lake belonging to King 'Sûdraka, where I formed a great affection for the daughter of a Flamingo named Karpûramanjarî. A traveller from a distant country arrived there one day, knocked at the palace gate, and said to the porter who admitted him: "I am a Râjaputra; my name is Vîravara, and I am seeking employment. I pray you procure me an audience with the King." He was therefore introduced to the King and said: "Sir, if your Highness has need of a servant, will you engage me and pay me wages." "What do you want by way of wages?" inquired the King. "Sir," he replied, "I require

400 pieces of gold a day." "And what weapons?" continued the King. "I have two arms," said the Râjaputra; "all I want is a sword." "It is not possible for me to hire you," answered the King. Vîravara bowed and went out from the King's presence. One of the ministers said: "Sir, take him on trial for four days, and gave him the wages he asks. You will then see whether he is worth them or not." So the King called him back and gave him the wages he asked, at the same time presenting him with some betel; for:

71 Betel is pungent, bitter, spicy, sweet, caustic, astringent, a remover of wind, antiphlegmatic, a vermifuge, a sweetener of the breath, a remover of impurities, an ornament to the mouth, a kindler of the flame of love. These are the thirteen qualities in betel, signifying what a follower should be—qualities hardly to be found even in paradise.

The King observed with great care the way in which Vîravara disposed of this money. Half he gave to the gods and the Brâhmans, a quarter to the poor and needy: and he spent the remaining quarter on food and amusements. After having disposed of his wages in this way, he used to watch day and night at the palace gate, sword in hand, and when the King commanded him he would return to his own house. It so happened that one dark night the King heard a sound of weeping, and called out, "Who is on guard at the gate?" "I, Vîravara, please your Majesty," he replied. The King ordered him to inquire into the cause of the weeping, and Vîravara departed in obedience to the King's orders. The King thought to himself: "I have sent this Râjaputra out into darkness that might be felt: this was not right; I will go and see what it all means." So the King, taking his sword, followed Vîravara outside the gate of the city.

When the Râjaputra arrived at the place whence the sound proceeded, he found a young and beautiful woman, magnificently adorned, weeping. He addressed her: "What is your name, and why are you weeping?" "I am the Fortune of King 'Sûdraka," she replied. "I have long lived very happily under his protection, but three day's hence the King will die, and the Queen will be the cause of his death. I shall lose my protector: therefore I weep." "And how," inquired Vîravara, "may all this be prevented?" She replied: "If you will sacrifice your own son, 'Saktidhara, to the goddess Durgâ, then the King will live for a hundred years, and I shall dwell in peace and happiness." Vîravara returned to his house, woke up his wife and his son, and told them the speech of Lakshmî. "Fortunate indeed am I," exclaimed 'Saktidhara joyfully, "that it should rest with me to save the prince's life. Why should there be any delay? It is a glory and an honour for me to offer up my life." The mother of 'Saktidhara also said: "It is an offering worthy of our family: otherwise how can we render a return to the King for the wages that we have received from him?" So saying, they all went together to the temple of Durgâ, and having worshipped the goddess, Vîravara said: "Divine goddess, let the great King Sûdraka be saved from destruction by virtue of this my offering," and cut off his son's head. Then the Râjaputra reflecting: "I have now repaid the King what I have received from him; life without my boy would be a grievous burden," slew himself. His wife, too, overcome with grief for the loss of her husband and son, followed his example.

When the King heard this he was filled with astonishment, and said:

72 Insignificant creatures like myself live and die: but one like him never has been, and never will be, in the world again.

What profit is my life and kingdom to me without him?" The King seized upon his sword to smite himself, when the goddess appeared and held his hand, saying: "Son, do nothing rashly! Thy kingdom shall stand firm." The King fell before her and said: "Neither life, nor fortune, nor kingdom is anything to me. If there is any compassion for me let me die, and by my death restore to life again this Râjpautra with his wife and son: otherwise I will follow them." "Go in peace," replied the goddess. "I am well pleased with thy piety and tenderness to this servant of thine; he shall live again with his wife and son."

So the Râjaputra, restored to life, together with his wife and son, went back again with them home. The King returned, too, unobserved by them, and laid down to sleep on the roof of his palace. Soon after he called out again to Vîravara, and questioned him as to the sound of weeping. Vîravara replied: "I found a woman weeping outside the gate, who vanished on seeing me: that is all I have to tell you." The King, astounded at the Râjaputra's answer, thought: "How can so admirable a servant be rewarded sufficiently? for:

73 He who is free from meanness should speak kindly. The hero should not be a boaster. The generous man should be a shower of bounty to the deserving. The confident man should be free from harshness. The great man has all these good qualities."

So, very early in the morning, the King called together his council, and having related all the events of the past night, gave to the Râjaputra the kingdom of Karnâṭa as a reward for his loyal service.

"A stranger, therefore," continued the King, "is by no means necessarily an enemy. Strangers, as other persons, are good, bad, and indifferent."

The Chakravâka replied:

74 "What kind of a minister is he who, at the king's order, commands that to be done which ought not to be done? Better that the king be angered than that his destruction should be brought about by a wrong order.

75 The king who is flattered by physician, priest, and minister, will very soon lose health, righteousness, and treasure.

76 What has been gained by one person through his virtue may be gained by me. But the barber who while seeking treasure in his

infatuation killed a beggar, was himself put to death."

"How came that about?" asked the King.

The minister Sarvajna said:

STORY X

In the city of Ayodhyâ there lived a Kshâtriya called Chûḍâmaṇi. He was exceedingly avaricious, and in his desire for money worshipped the god whose crescent is the half-moon. At last, after worship and penances, he had a dream, in which Kuvera, the god of wealth, appeared to him, and told him that after having been shaved he was to stand behind the door of his house early in the morning, and that a beggar would come into the courtyard: that he was to kill the beggar with blows from his stick, and that the beggar would immediately turn into a pit of gold, from which he would be a rich man for the rest of his life. The Kshâtriya did exactly as he had been bidden, and his dream came true to the letter. Now the barber who had come to shave him was a witness of all that happened, and he thought: "Well! this is an easy way to grow rich; I may as well try it myself." So he waited day after day, stick in hand, until one day a beggar came by, whom he killed with his stick, and the end of it was that he was arrested by the King's officers and beaten until he died. Therefore I say: What has been gained by one person through his virtue may be gained by me.

The King exclaimed :

77 "And pray how is the character of a stranger to be ascertained by the relation of all these old stories? Can you tell from them whether he is a disinterested friend or a double-dealing traitor?

Enough of this! We must attend to the matter in hand. Here is King Chitravarṇa actually encamped at the foot of Malaya; what is to be done now?" The Minister replied: "Sir, I hear from the spy who has just arrived that Chitravarṇa disregards the advice of his able minister the Vulture. I should imagine, therefore, that it would be possible to subdue him; for as it has been said:

78 The covetous: the cruel: the fickle: the liar: the heedless: the unstable: the stupid: the man who despises warriors: enemies of this kind are very easily overthrown.

Therefore, my advice is," continued the Chakravâka, "that the Sârasa and the other generals should be commanded to annihilate the enemy's forces wherever they find them—in the rivers—the mountains—the forests—and the roads, before he has been able to lay siege to our fortress; for it has been said:

79 The king should always take the enemy's army and discomfit them—when worn out by marches—weakened by hunger and thirst—straggling along in confusion and uncertainty.

Therefore the generals should follow up Chitravarṇa's force by day and night, and attack it as they have opportunity."

This scheme was therefore carried out, and a good many men of the enemy's army were killed. Chitravarṇa grew very despondent at the disasters which fell on his forces, and he said to his minister Dûradarśîn: "What is the meaning of this? Are you giving up your supervision of the army, or have I made any mistakes? For as it has been said:

80 Since we have not gained possession of the kingdom, there must be something amiss; For want of prudence destroys prosperity just as old age destroys beauty.

81 The clever man gains success: the man who eats wholesome food, health: the man who is healthy, ease: the diligent man, perfect knowledge: the man who is disciplined, righteousness, riches, and glory.

The Vulture answered: "Sir:

82 A king, though he have not knowledge himself, may gain glory from the advice of a wise man: as a tree growing near the river sucks up the water.

83 Great successes cannot be gained by the man who is simply brave, but who has no resources within himself: real success attends bravery and policy combined.

But your Majesty, looking only to the number and extent of your forces, has paid no attention to my advice: you have been harsh and unbending to your soldiers, and as a consequence these disasters have happened; for it is said:

84 Severity destroys happiness: winter, autumn—

the sun, darkness—ingratitude, good deeds —the presence of a friend, grief: good policy repairs disasters; bad policy overthrows prosperity.

"I reasoned with myself," continued Dûradarśîn, in this way. I said: 'Here is a prince—the King of the Peacocks. Surely he must have lost all understanding, or how could he make the moonlight of sound policy invisible through the firebrands of his own talk; for:

85 What can learning do for the man devoid of sense? What is the use of a mirror to the blind man?' Therefore, though I observed all that has happened, I kept silence."

Then King Chitravarṇa, perceiving his errors, addressed Dûradarśîn, with great respect. "Sir, the fault is all my own! But now tell me how I can retreat to the Vindhya mountains with those forces that I have left." The Vulture remained for a few minutes lost in thought, and then he replied: "I must try and find some remedy; for:

86 Anger should never be shown before the gods, before a spiritual teacher, before cattle, kings, Brâhmans, children, the old or the sick."

So he turned to the King with a smile and said: "Be not cast down: a way shall be found for your Majesty; for:

87 The skill of ministers is shown in repairing mistakes—of physicians in curing severe diseases; anyone can be wise when there are no difficulties.

88 People of small intelligence are easily baffled,

even in trifles. Men of wisdom launch out into arduous undertakings, and fail not in their purpose.

My advice is," continued Dûradarśîn, "to make an attack on the fortress, and then, after you have taken it, and gained honour and glory, I will lead your Majesty and the army back again to the Vindhya mountains." "But how," said the King, "can this be done with the very small force that we have left?" "Sir," answered the Vulture, "this shall be carried out; but if you desire to overcome the enemy and to take the fort, it is absolutely necessary that there should be no delay. The blockade of the fortress should begin at once." The spy who was in Chitravarṇa's army then returned to Hiraṇyagarbha and told him that an immediate attack on the fortress was to be expected. "The King," he said, "relying on the advice of the Vulture, is bringing up the remains of his army." "Well, Sarvajna, what is to be done now?" said the Flamingo. The Chakravâka replied: "We must carefully look over our forces and see what parts are efficient and what inefficient: and then, having picked out the most capable men in the army, your Majesty must give them gold, jewels, and other presents from the royal treasure; for it has been said:

89 The prince who will not misspend one single cowrie any more than a thousand pieces of gold; but who will, when the time arises, even freely dispense tens of millions—such a magnificent prince fortune will never desert.

90 On a sacrifice, on a wedding, at a time of distress, for the destruction of an enemy, on a glorious work, on the entertainment of friends, on favourite wives, on poor relations: there can be no excess in expenditure.

91 The fool through fear of a trifling expenditure ruins everything. A wise man does not refuse to accept a bale of merchandise because of the tax on it."

"But how," inquired the King, "can this extravagance be justified? For it has been said: 'A man should lay up his riches against a time of calamity.'" "Can misfortune ever attack the fortunate?" rejoined the Minister. "Fortune," replied the King, "is uncertain." The minister answered: "Sir, wealth that is hoarded is lost. Therefore I pray your Majesty to put aside these thoughts of avarice, and to reward your soldiers with honours and riches; for it has been said:

92 Soldiers—bound together by ties of mutual friendship—in high spirits—ready to sacrifice their lives—loyal—of good family—treated with marks of distinction—will overwhelm the enemy's host.

93 Brave soldiers, of loyal disposition, resolute, though only 500 in number, will vanquish a host.

94 There are three qualities which a king must possess: truth, bravery, and liberality. Without these he cannot escape reproach.

Ministers ought undoubtedly to be honoured:

95 A minister who is bound by the closest ties

and who rises and falls with his sovereign: such a minister is worthy of the fullest confidence.

96 Earth will open her treasury to the sovereign who is restrained, both in anger and in rejoicing, who keeps his expenditure within bounds, who treats his ministers with respect.

97 A king who understands the art of government should not visit those ministers with disgrace whose rise and fall is straitly bound up with the rise and fall of their lord.

98 Faithful and loyal ministers will hold out a helping hand to the sovereign who, blinded by rashness, is, as it were, overwhelmed in the ocean of difficulty."

Just at that moment Meghavarṇa, the Crow, arrived on the scene, and said: "Sir, the enemy are actually at the gate of the fortress. If your Majesty will allow me, I will sally forth and display my valour in return for your kindness towards me." "Certainly not," replied the Chakravâka; "if we are to go out and fight, what is the use of the fortress; besides:

99 An alligator, dangerous as he is, is harmless if he once leaves the water: a lion if he has once left the forest will certainly take up the habits of a jackal.

Let your Majesty," said the Minister, "go out yourself and view the battle; for:

100 A king, sending his forces in front, should incite them to battle by his presence. Even

a dog, when his master is by, has the courage of a lion."

On this they marched out to the gate of the fortress and met the enemy in deadly conflict.

Next morning King Chitravarṇa said to his Prime Minister, the Vulture : "Sir, now is the time for the performance of your promise." The Vulture returned : "Listen :

101 The fall of a fortress is said to be certain, when it cannot hold out any longer, when it is very small, when the commander is vicious or a fool, when it is unguarded, when it is garrisoned by cowards. That, however, is not the case with this fort ; still it may be taken, because :

102 There are four expedients by which a fort may be taken—bribery : siege : surprise : storming.

In this case I should advise the last expedient." Chitravarṇa heartily agreed with his minister's advice, and very early in the morning an attack was made by the besieging army on the four gates of the fort. At the same time the crows threw fire into every dwelling within the fortress. The soldiers of the garrison, attacked both from within and without, were thrown into a panic, and seeing the houses blazing shouted, "The fort is taken," and rushed into the pond ; for :

103 If a retreat (as it has been said) is determined upon, it should be made at once and without hesitation.

The Flamingo, being a quiet, easy-going monarch,

moved but slowly, accompanied by his commander-in-chief, the Sârasa, and was immediately surrounded by Chitravarṇa's forces led by the Cock.

Hiraṇyagarbha, perceiving his case to be hopeless, said to the Sârasa: "Your attachment to me must not involve you in my destruction. I can go no further; do you escape alone. Leave the fortress and make for the pond, and in conjunction with Sarvajna, the Prime Minister, make my son Chûrâmani king." "Sir," replied the Sârasa, "this must not be thought of for a minute. May your Majesty be victorious as long as the world shall last. I am the commander of your Majesty's fortress, and the enemy can only enter over my lifeless body.

104 A master, gentle and liberal—able to recognize his servant's merit, is a gift of fortune, an must not be forsaken."

"True," replied the King, "but:

105 It is just as hard to find a servant as upright, as skilled, as loyal as thou art."

The Sârasa replied:

106 "If the battle could be avoided, and there was no peril of death, then I might depart: but seeing that death is inevitable to every living being, why should cowardice throw a shadow over my glory?

107 In this world, as uncertain as the waves of the sea troubled by the breeze, the desire to sacrifice one's own life for the sake of another is the result of virtuous acts in a former existence.

Thou, O King, art our Master ; and thou must always be guarded :

108 When the king sleeps, the whole world sleeps, and wakes again at his waking, as the lotus at sunrise.

109 The ruler, the minister, the realm, the fortress, the treasury, the army, the ally, the whole body of the citizens, these are the parts which make up a kingdom.

But of all these the King is the chief."

Meanwhile the battle raged, and the Cock, making an attack on the Flamingo, wounded him with his spurs. The Sârasa came up hastily to the rescue, protecting the King with his own body, who escaped into the pool, and killed the Cock, pierced through and through by his long sharp beak. The Sârasa then fell surrounded by a multitude of the birds, and Chitravarṇa entered the fortress as conqueror. So the Peacock King, making himself master of the fort and all that it contained, marched forth at the head of his army, while the bards chanted hymns of victory.

The Princes at the conclusion of the story exclaimed : "Truly the Sârasa showed his honour and loyalty, saving his master at the sacrifice of his own life."

110 Cows bring forth young in their own likeness, only now and then a mighty horned lord of the herd.

Vishṇuśarman continued :

"May the hero inherit, with the spirits of the air as his companions, the paradise which his own valour has won ; for it has been said :

111 Brave and loyal servants, who in gratitude sacrifice their lives for their lords, enter paradise.

112 A warrior who, beset by enemies, dies fighting bravely, gains eternal happiness.

"So ends war," concluded Vishṇuśarman.

"And we are grateful to you for making us sharers in your wisdom," said the Princes.

"Then receive this, too," said Vishṇuśarman :

113 "May your Highnesses succeed to your father's throne, and may you never be harassed by war : but may your enemies, overthrown by the winds of prudent counsel, fly for refuge to the mountain caves."

END OF VIGRAHA

IV

SANDHI

PEACE

SANDHI

PEACE

THE Princes were again seated round Vishṇuśarman at the time of instruction, and they said:

"Sir! we have heard all about war, now tell us something about peace."

"Hear, then," he answered, "what I have to tell you about peace.

1 After the great battle between the two sovereigns, when the armies of both were almost annihilated, a treaty was drawn up between the Vulture and the Chakravâka."

"And what were the terms of it?" asked the Princes.

Vishṇuśarman continued:

STORY I

After a truce had been proclaimed, the Flamingo said to the Chakravâka, his Prime Minister: "Do you know who threw the fire into the fort? Was it one of the enemy, or one of our own men in league with him?" The Chakravâka replied: "Sir, your Majesty's disinterested friend,' Meghavarṇa the Crow, is no longer to be seen. He has apparently left with all his following. I should be inclined to guess that he had something to do with it." "It is all part of my bad luck," said the King sadly, after a little reflection ; "as it has been said :

2 This is the fault of fate : my ministers are not to blame. What has been carefully planned is often destroyed through evil destiny."

"It may be so," replied the Minister, "but you should also recollect that it has also been said :

3 An ignorant man falls into difficulties, and then, not perceiving that it is his own fault, rails at fate. Again :

4 He who takes no heed to the advice of friends who wish him well will perish like the foolish turtle that fell from the stick."

"How did that happen?" said the King.

The Chakravâka said :

STORY II

There is a pond in Magadhadeśa called Phullotpala, and in it lived two geese whose names were Sankata and Vikata. They had a friend called Kambugrîva, a turtle, who lived close by. One day some fishermen came to the pond and said : "We will stay the night here, and as soon as it is morning we will catch the fish and the turtles and whatever else there is in this pond." The Turtle heard what the fishermen had said, so he went and told his friends the Geese, and asked them what he had better do. They replied : "Time enough to think about that when this disaster has happened." "Not at all," answered the Turtle ; " I don't agree with you ; prevention is better than cure. There is the old proverb :

5 Anâgatavedhâtâ and Pratyutpannamati were lucky enough to escape, but Yadbhavishyat was caught and killed."

" And how was that ? " said the Geese.

The Turtle answered :

STORY III

Some fishermen once came to this pond, and held exactly the same kind of conversation as that which I have just listened to. There were three fish in the pond who heard them. One of them, whose name was Anâgatavedhâtâ, said : " Well, I am off ! " and without another word he left the pond. Pratyutpannamati said : " I have not quite made up my mind whether to go or stay. I shall wait here and see how things turn out before I decide. If anything does happen, I can then settle what is best to be done ; for it has been said :

6 A really wise man can repair a disaster which has happened, as the merchant's wife did, who disowned her lover before her husband's eyes."

"And pray how was that ? " inquired Yadbhavishyat.

Pratyutpannamati said :

STORY IV

A merchant called Samudradatta lived in Vikramapura. His wife Ratnaprabhâ was always running after the men servants, and making love to them ; for as it is said :

7 No one comes amiss to women : they are always wandering about, like cows in a forest, looking for fresh pasturage.

One day Samudradatta caught his wife kissing one of the men servants. Ratnaprabhâ, who was full of expedient, hastily turned to her husband and said : "My lord, the impudence of this servant of yours is unbounded : he actually eats the camphor, which has been provided for your use. His breath smells quite strong of it." For as the saying is :

8 Women eat twice as much as men : they are four times as cunning : six times as vicious : eight times as much given to falling in love.

When the servant heard this he pretended to be insulted, and exclaimed : "This is a pretty house to live in, when the mistress is always smelling the servants' breath !" He went off in a rage. However, he was persuaded to return by his master, who apologized for his wife's conduct, and promised that it should not occur again. Therefore I say : A really wise man can repair a disaster which has happened.

"Well !" said Yadbhavishyat :

9 "What will be—will be. What will not be—will not be.

This maxim is quite good enough for me."

In the morning the fishermen returned as they had determined, and they caught Pratyutpannamati. He laid quite still, and the fishermen, thinking he was dead, took him out of the net and threw him on the bank. He immediately bounded into the pond and vanished, but Yadbhavishyat was taken and killed.

"Therefore," continued the Turtle, "I must take immediate steps to see how I can get to another pond." "Of course, if you could do that," replied the Geese, "you would be safe enough, but that is just the difficulty. How are you going to cross the land?" "You might carry me through the air," answered the Turtle. "That doesn't seem practicable," replied the Geese. "Perfectly," said the Turtle; "all you have to do is to carry a stick between you in your beaks, and I will hang on to the middle of the stick. You could easily carry me like that." "Well," replied the Geese, "perhaps we could. Anyhow, we are quite willing to try; but recollect this:

10 A wise man in every scheme always allows for possible failure. A foolish crane had her young ones eaten before her eyes by the weasels."

"How was that?" said the Turtle.

The Geese said:

STORY V

In the north there is a mountain called Gridmakûṭa, and under it, on the banks of the Revâ, some cranes lived in a fig tree. At the foot of the same tree was the hole of a serpent, and the serpent used to devour the young cranes. An old bird, who heard the cranes lamenting this disaster, said: "I will tell you what to do. Get some fish, and lay them in a line from the serpent's hole to the hole of the weasel. The weasel will eat the fish; he will in consequence be led to the hole where the serpent lives. Between these two there is a deadly enmity, and the end of it will be that the serpent will be killed by the weasel."

The old crane did as she was advised, and the anticipated result followed. But the weasel, after having killed the serpent, heard the young cranes chirping in the tree, so he ate them up too. Therefore I say: A wise man in every scheme always looks for possible failure.

When the Geese had finished their story they continued: "While we are carrying you along hanging by your mouth to the stick, people are sure to make some remarks. If you open your mouth to answer them, you will fall from the stick, and there will be an end of you. Therefore we think you had better stop here." "You must think me a fool," exclaimed the Turtle, with some wrath; "I will not utter a word." "Very good," replied the Geese. "So be it, then!" and they proceeded to execute the plan. They had not got far on their journey when some herdsmen saw the Turtle being borne along in the air by the Geese. The herdsmen rushed in pursuit calling out: "Hullo! here is a funny thing! A turtle being carried along by two geese." Said one of the herdsmen: "He is sure to tumble down before long. When he does, we will take him home and cook him." "No," said the second, "we will cook him and eat him here." The third man agreed with neither, but said: "Let us cook him and eat him near the pond."

The Turtle, hearing himself disposed of in this off-hand way, could not restrain his wrath any longer, but shouted out: "You villains! you shall eat ashes!" No sooner had he opened his mouth than he fell from the stick, and the herdsmen killed him and ate him. Therefore I say: He who takes no heed to the advice of friends who wish him well, will perish like the foolish turtle.

The Chakravâka had hardly finished these stories when the Crane, who had been sent out to get intelligence, came back and said: "Your Majesty may remember that I advised all strangers to be dismissed from the fortress at the very beginning of the siege. You did not take my advice. The consequence was that Meghavarṇa the Crow, who was in the pay of the Vulture Dûradarśîn, contrived the burning of the fortress."

The King sighed and said:

11 "He who confides in enemies through respect for them, or because they have rendered him assistance, is like a man who has gone to sleep on the top of a tree and fallen through the branches."

"That this is true is quite certain," continued the Crane, "for after the burning of the fortress Chitravarṇa showed the greatest favour to Meghavarṇa, and ordered him to be crowned and anointed King of Karpûradvîpa ; for :

12 It is not right that the labour of a servant should be passed by without recompense. Such a one should be rewarded with liberality, and by kindly feeling both in word and in look."

"Your Majesty hears," said the Chakravâka, "what the spy has said." "Well," said the King, "and what next?" The spy continued: "The Vulture said: 'This is not at all prudent, your Majesty. Meghavarṇa may have some mark of royal favour shown him, but not this that you propose ; for :

13 If he be once invested with this high position, how will it be possible to deprive him of it? Besides, showing kindness to persons of low character is like writing on the sand.

An ignoble man should never be allowed to attain to an exalted place. It has been said :

14 When a low-minded person has gained a post of honour, he desires to get rid of the master who has raised him: as the mouse who attained the state of a tiger wished to kill the saint.'

'How was that?' said Chitravarṇa.

The Vulture related the following story :

STORY VI

Once upon a time a great Saint lived in the forest of Gautama. One day he rescued a mouse from the clutches of a crow, who was going to kill and eat it, and taking it to his hermitage brought it up on rice. Soon after he saw the mouse pursued by a cat; so the Saint, by the power which he had gained in penances, turned the mouse into a fine strong cat. Some time passed, and the cat was worried by a dog. The Saint carried out a second metamorphosis and changed the cat into a dog. A tiger next appeared on the scene, and to save the dog from being eaten by the tiger he turned it into a tiger. The Saint, however, treated the tiger exactly as though he were still a mouse, and the people who saw him said: "Look! there is the tiger. He was once a mouse, but the Saint, by the exercise of his power, has changed him into a tiger."

This made the tiger feel very uncomfortable, and he kept thinking to himself: "As long as this Saint lives, the story of my disgraceful origin will never be forgotten." So at last he made up his mind to take the first opportunity of killing the Saint. The latter, however, by his spiritual power, was able to penetrate the tiger's design, and anticipated its execution by turning to him and saying: "Go back to your former shape and be a mouse." No sooner had the Saint uttered the words than the tiger found himself reduced to the insignificant condition from which he had sprung, and was condemned to pass the rest of his days as a mouse.

Wherefore I say: When a low-minded person has gained a post of honour, he desires to get rid of the master who has raised him.

"Besides, your Majesty must recollect," continued the Minister, "that it is not always so easy to turn a man out after you have placed him in a position of influence.

15 A stupid crane, after devouring great quantities of fish, great and small, was seized and killed by a crab as a punishment for his greediness."

"How did that happen?" said the King.

The Minister said:

STORY VII

There is a pond in the Malva country called Padmagarbha. In this pond lived an aged Crane who had grown very decrepid, and presented a deplorable appearance as he stood moping in the water without attempting to find any food. A Crab observed him, and keeping at a respectful distance, asked him why he stood in that dejected state. "My worthy friend," replied the Crane, "I live on fish: but I hear that all the fish in this pond are going to be caught and killed. It is quite clear, therefore, that my days are numbered, and so I shall not take any more trouble to get food." The fish in the pond heard this conversation; they therefore debated among themselves what they had better do, and since, on this occasion at least, there was nothing to fear from their natural enemy the Crane, they thought it might be well to ask his advice; for as it is said:

16 An alliance should be formed with an enemy who will help, rather than with a friend who will hinder, for help and hindrance is the respective characteristic of both.

So the fish went in a body to the Crane and said: "Sir, we have heard of our impending destruction: we have come to ask your advice. How shall we escape?" "Easily enough," answered the Crane. "Go to another pond. I will take you there one by one." The fish, terrified at what looked like certain death to them, gladly consented to accept the Crane's services; so he took them out of the pond one at a time and ate them, always coming back and saying to the remaining fish: "Your friend reached the other pond in safety." At last a Crab came up and said: "My worthy Crane, I wish you would take me to this pond." The Crane assented very willingly, for he thought that the crab would make him an excellent meal; so he picked him up and carried him to the same place as that to which he had taken the fish. When they arrived there, the first thing that attracted his notice was the number of fish bones with which the ground was covered. He immediately perceived that he had been trapped, and he said to himself: "Well, I have been nicely caught. I must use all my wits to get out of this; for:

17 Danger is only to be feared as long as it is at a distance. As soon as it comes near, it must be met bravely.

18 When a brave man is attacked and sees no way out of the danger, he shows a bold front to the enemy and perishes in the conflict."

So the Crab, with these reflections, seized the Crane by the throat and held on until he was strangled.

"Therefore it is clear that a man of low character once taken up, is not easily shaken off." "You are indeed a minister of consummate wisdom," said King Chitravarṇa to the Vulture; "but I think I have a plan that will answer. You know Karpûra-dvîpa is a very rich country. Now Meghavarṇa might be made king, and at the same time might send us all its productions as attribute. In that way he would get the honour and we should get all the profit."

Dûradarśîn smiled and said: "Your Majesty:

19 He who congratulates himself on the success of a plan, the end of which lies in the future, will be disappointed like the Brâhman who broke the pots."

"How was that?" said the King.

Dûradarśîn related the following.

STORY VIII

In Devîkoṭṭa lived a Brâhman called Devaśarman. One fine day he bought a pot of flour, and as he was carrying it home he became overwhelmed with the heat, and laid down to rest in a potter's shed, which was full of earthen pots. As he lay resting in the shed, he thought to himself: "I shall sell this flour at a good profit, and with that I shall buy a quantity of pots, and make a good deal of money out of them. With this I shall lay in a stock of betel nuts, cloth, and various other goods, and so by dealing in these articles I shall amass a tidy fortune. I shall then marry four wives: one of them will be young and beautiful, and on her I shall lavish all my affection. The other three will be exceedingly jealous, and there will be a great deal of disturbance in the house. When that comes about, I shall thrash them all round with this stick," and so saying he hit out with the stick which he had in his hand, and broke not only his own pot, whereby he lost all the flour, but also a great many of the pots in the shed. The potter heard the noise and came in. When he saw the damage that had been done, he fell upon the Brâhman in a rage, beat him severely, and kicked him out of the shed.

Therefore I say: He who congratulates himself on the success of a plan, the end of which lies in the future, will be disappointed.

The King was at a loss what to do, and taking Dûradarśîn aside privately, said: "Pray give me your advice." The Vulture said: "Sir:

20 The minister of a king inflated with pride is in somewhat the same condition as the driver of a restive elephant: both are blamed for the vagaries of another.

Your Majesty may, perhaps, recollect the capture of the fort. It was not taken by the overwhelming strength of our forces, but by a device of your Majesty's own surpassing skill." "Not at all," replied the King, "the device and the skill were yours." "Then," continued the Vulture, "if you will take my advice in this case, you will return home immediately. The rainy season is coming on, and if we have to fight the enemy with our diminished forces, it is extremely likely that we shall get the worst of it, and then a retreat will be impossible, or at least, very difficult. For the sake of our own ease and credit let us make peace and go. We have taken the fortress and gained a good deal of glory: let us be satisfied with that. Such is my opinion; for:

21 The minister who puts his duty before his sovereign and tells him the truth, whether it be pleasing or unpleasing, is a valuable servant.

22 Peace should be sought even with an equal: for victory in a fight is always doubtful. Nothing should be left to chance. So says Vrihaspatî.

23 No one but an idiot would expose himself, his kingdom, his friends, his reputation, to the risk and uncertainty of a battle.

24 Sometimes in a fight both sides are destroyed. Did not Sunda and Upasunda, though equal in strength, both perish?"

"How was that?" said Chitravarṇa.

Dûradarśîn proceeded:

STORY IX

In bygone times there were two giants, whose names were Sunda and Upasunda. For a long time they worshipped the deity whose crest is the half-moon, and performed many a severe penance; for the desire had seized on them of gaining the sovereignty of the three worlds. At last the god, pleased with their devotion, appeared to them and said : "Choose what I shall give you." When they essayed to answer they were unable to control their words, and under the overpowering influence of Saraśvatî, though they meant one thing they said another, and returned answer : "If our lord be pleased with us, then let him give us his own Parvatî." Now Parvatî was the wife of the moon-crested deity ; and though the god was full of wrath at the request, he did not like to go back from his promise, or refuse the giants what they had asked, so he gave them Parvatî. Immediately a contention arose between them whose she should be. The dispute waxed hot, and at last they agreed to refer the matter for decision to an arbitrator. Just at that moment the moon-crested deity appeared before them in the form of an aged Brâhman, and to him they agreed to refer the dispute. They said : "Sir, to which of us two does this damsel belong, for we have both gained her by our strength ?"

The Brâhman replied :

25 A Brâhman is honoured for his wisdom :
A Kshâtriya for his valour :
A Vaiśya for his riches :
A 'Sûdra for his service to the twice born :
You are Kshâtriyas, therefore you must fight."

They both exclaimed : "You have well said !" and immediately acted on his advice ; when, being of exactly equal strength, they slew each other with a mutual blow. Therefore I say : Peace should be sought even with an equal.

26 A truthful man, and a just man: an ignoble man: a man who has many brothers: a strong man: a man who has been victorious in many fights. With these six peace should be made.

27 A truthful man, when he has made peace, does not change, because he holds his word inviolable. A man of noble mind, even if his life is in danger, will never condescend to an unworthy action.

28 Everyone will fight for a just man when he is attacked. The just man will be hardly overthrown, for he has gained the love of his people.

29 Peace should be made even with an ignoble man if ruin seems impending: and when by doing so time may be gained.

30 Just as a bamboo stem cannot be cut down when it is hedged about by impenetrable thorns, so the man who is hedged about by his brothers cannot be cut off.

31 It is no use to contend against a strong man. Clouds will not float against the wind.

32 The man who has been victorious in many battles is even as the son of Jamadagni: he is absolute master of everything.

33 The enemies of one who makes an alliance with him will speedily be subdued.

"Therefore," continued the Vulture, "since the Flamingo King is endued with many excellent qualities, we ought to make peace with him."

When the spy had finished, the Chakravâka said:

"You have done well. Now go back again to the court of Chitravarṇa, find out what further news there is, and come back and tell us."

"Sir," said Hiraṇyagarbha when the spy had gone on his mission, "I wish you would tell me who ought *not* to be made peace with."

The Minister replied: "Your Majesty:

34–52 (condensed)

Make no peace with a sovereign who is a child, for he knows not the difference between peace and war, neither will his subjects follow him.

Make no peace with an old man, nor with a sick man, for they are both incapable of exertion, and are despised by their people.

Make no peace with an outcast from his own kin, for they will join the enemy against him.

Make no peace with a coward, or with one whose followers are cowards. They are both lost.

Make no peace with a covetous man, for his soldiers will not fight because he withholds their pay.

Make no peace with him whose officers are disloyal, for when the battle comes they will desert him.

Make no peace with him who is the slave of sensuality, for he will be easily overcome.

Make no peace with the man who knows not his own mind, for his ministers will care nothing for his interest.

Make no peace with the man who despises the gods and the Brâhmans, for he will wither away: nor with the man who is the victim of fate, for he shall perish.

Make no peace with the man who looks on fate alone as the author of prosperity or adversity, for he will not bestir himself.

Make no peace with the man whose country is smitten by famine, for he must yield of himself: nor with the man whose army is in disorder, for his soldiers will not fight.

Make no peace with the man who has a host of enemies, for he will be destroyed like a pigeon surrounded by hawks.

Make no peace with the man who fights at the wrong time and place, for he will be destroyed even as a crow is killed by an owl on a dark starless night.

Make no peace, and form no alliance, with the dishonourable or the untruthful man: for though he may make a treaty, he will not keep it.

Yet farther than this: Knowledge—Skill—Counsel—Expedients. The sovereign and his ministers who would be victorious must be well versed in all these; for:

53 Fortune is a fickle jade—not to be won at the price of life—always on the side of him who has the most skill and knowledge; and it has been said:

54 He who shares his wealth equally with others—whose spies are adroit, whose counsel is hidden, and whose speech is always kindly—he may rule over the whole earth.

But even if peace were proposed by the Vulture," continued the Chakravâka, "great and influential minister as he is, I hardly think that Chitravarṇa, elated by victory, would consent to it. I should therefore propose to induce our ally the Sârasa Mahâbala, the King of Sinhaladvîpa, to stir up a rebellion in Karpûradvîpa."

"Very good," answered Hiraṇyagarbha. A crane called Vichitra was therefore dispatched to the King of Sinhaladvîpa with a letter. Just at that moment the spy returned who had been sent to the court of Chitravarṇa to gather intelligence.

"If your Majesty will listen," he said, "I have further news for you, for I have heard what has passed in the council of King Chitravarṇa.

In the course of the discussion as to whether a peace should be proposed to your Majesty or not, the Vulture said: 'Sir, let us inquire of Meghavarṇa, the Crow, as to Hiraṇyagarbha's character and disposition—whether he would be likely to listen to proposals for peace or not. For Meghavarṇa was at Hiraṇyagarbha's court for a long while.'

So Meghavarṇa was sent for, and he was asked what he thought of Hiraṇyagarbha, and what sort of a minister was the Chakravâka. He answered: 'Sir, Hiraṇyagarbha is a king truthful and generous in disposition,—the equal of Yudhishthira himself, and a minister equal in skill and ability to Sarvajna the Chakravâka does not exist.' 'How, then,' inquired the King, 'were you able to deceive Hiraṇyagarbha?'

Meghavarṇa smiled and said:

55 "What skill is required to deceive one who reposes confidence in you? It does not require a hero to kill a child which is asleep on its mother's lap.

The truth is, that the Minister saw through me at once, but the king fell a victim to his own kindly disposition. Therefore he was deceived; for:

56 He who judging by himself looks on a deceitful man as a speaker of the truth, will be taken in as the Brâhman was in the affair of the goat.'

'How was that?' inquired the King.

Meghavarṇa said:

STORY X

In Gauḍa there lived a Brâhman named Yajnaśarma. One day he went to a neighbouring village and bought a goat for sacrifice. As he was returning home, carrying the goat on his shoulders, three scoundrels met him. They saw the Brâhman carrying the goat in the distance, and made up their minds to get possession of it. So they exercised their ingenuity and posted themselves along the roadside, at some distance apart from each other. When the Brâhman came up to the first rogue the man accosted him and exclaimed: "Reverend sir! how is it that you are carrying an unclean beast like a dog on your shoulder?" The Brâhman replied: "My friend! you are quite mistaken. This is not a dog, but a goat which I have bought for a sacrifice." The Brâhman then resumed his journey, and soon after, at a short distance, met the second rogue, who addressed him in exactly the same way as the first. On hearing this the Brâhman felt a little uncomfortable, and putting the goat down on the ground, looked it carefully over. However, it clearly seemed to him to be a goat, so he picked it up again and proceeded on his journey, though he did not feel quite so confident as before ; for :

57 The mind even of the good may be perverted by the advice of the evil : and he who confides in evil men may perish like Chitrakarṇa.

The King said : "And how was that?"

Meghavarṇa continued :

STORY XI

In a certain forest there lived a lion called Madotkaṭa, who had three followers—a tiger, a jackal, and a crow. One day when they were prowling about they came across a camel that had strayed away from a caravan, and they asked him where he had come from. He told them in answer his whole history, and so they took him to the lion, who promised to protect him, and gave him the name of Chitrakarṇa. The camel then became one of the lion's followers. Now after a time the lion became ill, and in consequence of the excessive quantity of rain they found it extremely difficult to get food. The tiger, the jackal, and the crow thereupon formed a scheme to make their master the lion kill Chitrakarṇa ; for they said among themselves : "What have we to do with this eater of thorns?" The Tiger said: "But will this be possible? for our lord has given him a promise of protection." The Crow replied: "At such a time as this, when our master is absolutely perishing with hunger, he will even commit a crime.

58 A mother, tormented with hunger, will cast off even her own child: a serpent tormented with hunger will eat even her own eggs. What crime will not the hungry man perpetrate? The famine-stricken have no pity."

So they went in a body to the Lion. The Lion said: "What have you brought me to eat?" "Sir," answered the Crow, "we have done our best, but we can find nothing to eat." "Then," said the Lion, "what are we to live on? All our means are gone." The Crow replied: "It is your Highness's own self which has brought us into this state of destitution. You will not take what is actually in your own power." "What food have I possession of?" answered the Lion. "Chitrakarṇa," said the Crow in a whisper. The Lion bowed to the ground in token of reverence, and said: "Oh! but I have given him my word, and a promise of security. How then can I go against that? for:

59 The gift of land, of cattle, of money, even of food—there is no gift as great as that which is called the greatest of all—the gift of security.

60 He who protects a fugitive gains a blessing great as that obtained from the Aśvamedha sacrifice which fulfils every wish."

The Crow said to his friends, the Tiger and the Jackal: "It is quite clear our master will not kill him: perhaps we may get him to offer himself." The Crow proposed this to the Lion, who offered no objection.

So the Crow, watching for the opportunity, went along with the rest of the Lion's followers, before their master, and said: "Sir, we have taken all pains, but we can find no food. Your Highness is worn out by starvation. Therefore I offer myself to you for a meal; for:

61 The whole state rests upon the sovereign and has its roots in him. Men may bestow their labour on trees which have root to some purpose."

"My faithful follower," replied the Lion, "I would rather die than commit such a crime as you suggest." The Jackal made the same offer, and he was followed by the Tiger, who both were met with a refusal in similar terms. Chitrakarṇa, the Camel, thinking that this offer was a mere matter of form, confidently made it on his own account; but he speedily found out his mistake, for no sooner were the words out of his mouth than the Tiger fell upon him, tore him to pieces, and they all ate him up. Therefore I say: The mind even of the good may be perverted by the advice of the evil, and he who confides in them perishes.

"The Brâhman, then," continued Meghavarṇa (concluding the story of the Brâhman and the goat), "came up to the third rogue, who addressed him exactly in the same manner as the other two.

The Brâhman could no longer resist, and so, convinced that he must have been mistaken, he threw down what he believed to be a dog, and went through a course of purification. Meanwhile the three scoundrels took the goat home and feasted upon it. Therefore I say: He who judging by himself looks on a deceitful man as the speaker of the truth, will be deceived."

When Meghavarṇa had concluded, the King turned to him and said: "But how did you manage to live so long among enemies, and how did you manage to gain their confidence?" "Your Majesty," replied the Crow, "one who has his master's interest at heart—or his own ends to serve—will do anything; for:

62 People carry wood on their heads, but yet they mean to burn it. A river washes the roots of a tree, but all the time it is undermining it.

It has been said:

63 A wise man to serve his own ends will carry even his enemy on his shoulder, as the old serpent did who destroyed the frogs."

"Pray how did that happen?" inquired the King. Meghavarṇa related the following:

STORY XII

In a garden which had gone out of cultivation lived a Serpent called Mandavisarpa. He was so old and decrepid that he lay on the banks of a pond quite unable to find food for himself. A Frog saw him, and keeping at a safe distance, said to him: "Why do you lie there all day without trying to get something to eat?" The Serpent answered: "Go your ways! Why should you wish to hear the story of such a wretch as I am?" The Frog was filled with curiosity, and said: "I am very desirous to hear it; I pray you tell it me." The Serpent replied: "My friend, a learned Brâhman, whose name was Kauṇḍinya, once lived here in Brahmapura. He had a son, about twenty years of age, a very model of every virtue, and one day I—under the influence of an evil fate—bit him, so that he died. Kauṇḍinya happened to come by, and seeing his son, who was called Suśîla, lying dead upon the ground, was so overcome with grief that he fainted. Then all his kinsmen and relations who lived in Brahmapura came and sat down beside him; for it has been said:

64 The man who will feast with us and mourn with us—who will follow us in famine or in war, to the king's gate, and to the place of burial: he is a kinsman indeed.

Then a certain Kapila, a proficient in religious lore, spoke out and said: 'O Kauṇḍinya, you are a fool in that you make this lament; for:

65 We are clasped to the bosom by mortality—first as a nurse, then as a mother. Why should there be all this grief?

66 Where are the great rulers of the earth, with their guards, their armies, their chariots? To this day the earth bears witness to their departure.

67 Each day the outward form wastes away imperceptibly, like an unbaked jar standing in water. Until the jar has disappeared, it is not known that it is vanishing.

68 As a victim approaches the altar, step by step, so death comes nearer day by day to every living being.

69 Youth, beauty, life, riches, power, friends, all pass away. A wise man fixes not his hopes on these.

70 As a plank of timber may meet another plank in the ocean and then part asunder again, even so is the meeting of men in this world.

71 As a traveller rests in the shade, and then rises again and passes on, even so is the life of men in the world.

72 Why should we lament over a body which returns to the five elements out of which it was formed, finding once more its own birthplace?

73 As many ties a man forms in this world, dear to the soul, so many thorns of sorrow he plants in his heart.

74 No man may gain an abiding place in this world for himself: how much less for another.

75 Where there is union there must also be separation; where there is birth there must also be death.

76 The end of union with beloved friends—delightful at the time—is as if a man had taken poison.

77 As the rivers flow onward and never turn back

again, so do night and day go by, carrying mortals away.

78 Union with good men giving the sweetest flavour to our enjoyment in the world, is joined to a burthen of troubles, because the end of it is separation.

79 Therefore wise men abstain from forming friendship with the good, because there is no cure for the heart wounded by the dagger of separation.

80 Though Sagara and other mighty kings have performed wonderful works, there is no trace left either of them or of their deeds.

81 A man perpetually thinking on death with his terrible scourge, though he be of keen intelligence, yet all his energies become slack, like a leather thong soaked in water.

82 From the very first moment that he takes up his abode in the womb, the man of valour marches along day by day unfaltering to death.

Therefore reflect on what life in the world really is : for such sorrow as this is but the result of ignorance.

83 Ignorance is the cause of sorrow, not bereavement : if bereavement were the cause, sorrow would increase : for why should it depart?

Therefore, sir, be calm, and dismiss all thought of sorrow.

84 The only unfailing cure for the wounds which penetrate, as it were, even our inmost parts, is not to think upon the griefs which cause them.'

Kauṇḍinya, waking as if from sleep at these words, started up and exclaimed: 'Enough of dwelling in this house which is hell to me: I will go to the forest.'

Kapila answered and said:

85 'Even in a forest the unrestrained are subject to evil. The house of him whose passions are held in check, and whose deeds are blameless, *is* the forest. Restraining the senses in a house is penance.

86 Though a man be in affliction, he should always abide in his own calling,—performing his duty,—evenminded under all conditions. Outward observances are not righteousness.

87 Those who eat only to live: those who marry only for the sake of offspring: those who speak only to declare the truth: such as these overcome the difficulties of life.

88 Thou thyself art a river: self-restraint is thy place of sacred pilgrimage: truth is thy water: morality is thy bank: pity is thy waves. Here perform thy rites of purification, O son of Pâṇḍu, for the outward washing of water alone shall not purify thy inner self.

89 To quit this world is a blessing—a world overwhelmed with the pains of birth, death, old age, and disease.

90 Pain has a real existence, ease has no real existence: that is clear, for the word ease simply means the alleviation of pain.'

'Indeed, this is true,' said Kauṇḍinya."

The Serpent continued : "Then Kauṇḍinya, who was overwhelmed with grief, cursed me : 'From this day forward you are condemned to carry frogs.' Kapila, hearing the curse, said to Kauṇḍinya : 'At present thou art not able to receive advice, because thy heart is filled full of grief. Nevertheless, hear what I tell thee :

91 The society of men should be avoided with thy whole soul : but if it cannot be given up, then associate with the good, for that is even as healing medicine.'

Then Kauṇḍinya, the fire of whose grief was allayed by the amrit of Kapila's advice, according to the sacred order took up the staff of a pilgrim, while I wait here to fulfil the Brâhman's curse, and to carry frogs.

So the Frog returned to Jâlapâda, the King of the Frogs, and told him what he had heard.

Jâlapâda then came himself, and the Serpent took the King of the Frogs on his back, and gave him a very pleasant ride. Next day Jâlapâda came again, but the Serpent was hardly able to move, and went along very slowly. Jâlapâda asked him the reason. The Serpent said : "I am weak and unable to move from want of food." The King of the Frogs said : "You are very welcome to the frogs, if you want something to eat." The Serpent was delighted at the offer, which he gladly accepted, and so he ate up all the frogs in the pond one be one, finishing with his Majesty the King. Therefore I say : A wise man to serve his own ends will carry even his enemy on his shoulder.

Meghavarṇa concluded his story by saying: "However, your Majesty, if it please you, we have heard enough of old stories. Now as to King Hiraṇyagarbha—he is a worthy sovereign; let peace be made with him. That is my opinion." "What an idea!" returned King Chitravarṇa, "such a thing is quite out of the question! He has been absolutely defeated by me—so if he is content to exist as my vassal, well and good; otherwise the war must be continued." Just at that moment the Parrot returned from Jambudvîpa with the news that the King of Sinhaladvîpa claimed the sovereignity over Jambudvîpa, and had asserted his claim by invading the country. King Chitravarṇa was violently disturbed, and exclaimed over and over again: "What? what? Tell it me again." The Parrot repeated with more detail what he had already said. The Vulture thought to himself: "Well, after all, the minister Chakravâka has not done badly." The King burst into a fury: "Just let him wait a bit! I will go and destroy him root and branch." Dûradarśîn only smiled and said:

92 "A sound like thunder to no purpose is as unmeaning as an autumn cloud. A great man does not tell his enemies what he means to do, or what he does *not* mean to do.

93 A king should not contend with many enemies at once. Even a huge serpent is infallibly destroyed by a number of insects.

Please, your Majesty, it is impossible for us to retreat homewards without making peace. If we do the enemy will attack us in the rear.

94 The foolish man who without consideration gives way to anger, will be sorry for it, as the Brâhman who killed the mongoose."

"How did that happen?" said the King.

Dûradarśîn continued :

STORY XIII

In the city of Ujjayinî lived a Brâhman called Mâdhava. His wife, who belonged to the same caste, had recently brought forth a son, and she went to perform her ceremonial purification, leaving her infant son in charge of her husband. She had hardly gone when the Brâhman was sent for by the King, who wanted him to come and perform the Pârvanaśrâddha. The Brâhman, who was extremely poor, thought to himself: "If I don't go at once, someone else will be got to perform this Pârvanaśrâddha ; for it has been said :

95 When a work has to be done : when a present has to be received, or to be given : in each case delay destroys the virtue either of the work or of the gift.

But there is no one to look after the child, so what can I do? Well, I have a mongoose which has been brought up as if it were my own son. I will get it to look after the child in my absence." The Brâhman did so, and obeyed the King's summons. Presently a black snake was seen coming near with the intention of killing and devouring the child. The mongoose, who was on the look out, fell upon the snake, killed it, and tore it in pieces. Soon after the Brâhman returned. The first thing that he saw was the mongoose, who came to meet him with his mouth and paws covered with blood, and who rolled at his feet by way of greeting. The Brâhman, without further consideration, hastily concluding that the mongoose had eaten the child, killed it at once. Going a step further he found the child sleeping in the cradle, with the black snake dead beside him. Too late he recognized his mistake, and was overwhelmed with grief. Therefore I say: The foolish man who, without consideration, gives way to anger, will be sorry for it as the Brâhman was who killed the mongoose. Further:

96 Passion, wealth, covetousness, envy, pride, rashness: these six vices man should subdue; he should cast them off if he would attain happiness.

"Oh!" said the King; "so this is your opinion, is it?"

"It is," replied the Vulture; for:

97 Knowledge of precedent in matters of importance, deliberation, accurate knowledge, firmness, secrecy: these are the qualifications essential for a minister.

98 A man should not act hastily: want of consideration is the source of the greatest calamities. Good fortune, which naturally follows merit, is the companion of him who acts with discrimination.

If, then, my opinion is worth anything, let your Majesty make peace and go home again; for:

99 Though the means for carrying out the matter in hand may be various; after all the great point is a successful issue brought about by negotiation."

"Well," said the King, "and how do you propose to attain this?" "Sir," replied the Minister, "there will be no difficulty; for:

100 A bad man is like an earthen pot—easily broken, difficult to mend:

A good man is like a golden jar, broken with difficulty, easily mended.

101 An ignorant man it is just possible to conciliate; a learned and intelligent man it is easy to win over: but Brâhma himself cannot convince the man who is absolutely ignorant of everything.

Now King Hiraṇyagarbha is specially wise and intelligent, and his minister Sarvajna is a man of genius: I learnt all this long ago from Meghavarṇa, and communication with them has proved it to be true.

102 The good qualities of those who are absent must be judged by their actions, and by the results of their actions the character of these persons must be estimated."

The King broke in: "There! the matter has been discussed enough: do what is necessary."

Dûradarśîn thereupon started on a mission to the fort, with the intention of making proposals of peace to Hiraṇyagarbha. News of his arrival was immediately brought to the Flamingo. On hearing it, he exclaimed: "Chakravâka! Some daring person is coming here again to do us a mischief." "Your Majesty," answered Sarvajna with a smile, "not at all! You need have no anxiety. Dûradarśîn is a most noble-minded person. This, unfortunately, is the normal condition of dull-witted people; at one time they have no mistrust even of an enemy, at another they are afraid of every one; for:

103 A cunning goose one night, looking for lotus shoots in a pond, was deceived by the reflexion of the stars; so even in the daytime he would not bite at the water lily, thinking it was a star. In like manner, a person who has been once deceived, is looking out for deception even in the truth.

104 The mind which has been wronged by the wicked has no confidence even in the good. A child who has been burnt by scalding milk will not eat curds until he has blown upon it.

Therefore," continued Sarvajna, "let a present be got ready for the Minister, consisting of jewels and such like things, according to your Majesty's position, as a mark of respect." The Minister's suggestion was carried out, and the Vulture Dûradarśîn was received in great state by Sarvajna at the entrance of the fort. He was then introduced to King Hiraṇyagarbha, when a throne was set for him in the King's presence. When Dûradarśîn had taken his seat, Sarvajna approached him with great respect and said: "Sir, this kingdom is yours: do with it as you will." King Hiraṇyagarbha also addressed Dûradarśîn in terms of respect. The Vulture replied: "I gladly accept your salutations. But what need is there of words; for:

105 A covetous man should be met with money; an unbending man with humility: one should humour the desires of a fool, but an intelligent man should be addressed with truth.

106 A friend should be received with kindness: relations with affectionate haste: women and servants with gifts and honour: all men with courtesy.

Therefore," continued Dûradarśîn, "our desire is to make peace and be gone." "But on what terms," said the Chakravâka, "can peace be made?" "What kind of peace," said the Flamingo, "will you accept?" "Peace," answered Dûradarśîn, "may be made on many and various conditions, but I should suggest the peace made in friendship and conciliation—resting in mutual amity; the peace which men call the Golden."

"You, sirs," said Hiraṇyagarbha, "are great and wise ministers. Advise me, then, what I ought to do in this present case."

Dûradarśîn replied: "It is said:

107 Who would commit a crime for the sake of a body that will perish sooner or later by the pains of anxiety or disease?

108 The existence of living beings is as fleeting as the moonbeams that tremble on the water.

Knowing this, a man should ever act uprightly.

109 Seeing that the world changes in a moment

like the mirage, let a man, for the sake of righteousness and of peace, ever associate with the good.

My advice, then, is that righteousness and truth be followed; for:

110 If a thousand aśvamedha sacrifices were weighed in the balance with truth, truth would far outweigh the sacrifices.

Let, therefore, the Peace which is called Golden be ratified between these two monarchs, preceded by the oath named Truth." "Let it be so," answered Sarvajna. Then Dûradarśîn was honoured with gifts of raiment and gold, and went away rejoicing with the Chakravâka to the Peacock King. By the advice of the Vulture, a conference was held between Chitravarṇa and Sarvajna, and after the Minister had been loaded with honour and presents, the Golden Peace was concluded between them, and the Chakravâka returned to Hiraṇyagarbha.

Dûradarśin then addressed Chitravarṇa: "Sir, our object has been gained: let us return in peace to our home in the Vindhya Mountains."

"Now," said Vishṇuśarman to the Princes, "I have told your Highnesses all: what more would you know?" "Sir," answered the Princes, "you, through your goodness and learning, have taught us all the round of our kingly duties: we have learnt our lesson, and are satisfied." "That is well," replied Vishṇuśarman. "Now hear what I have to say in conclusion.

111 May happiness and peace ever be the lot of virtuous kings : may the good ever be free from calamity : may the glory of the righteous ever increase : may skilful policy, like a loving woman, ever cling to the necks and kiss the lips of ministers : and may joy, increasing day by day, be to all people."

END OF SANDHI

END OF HITOPADESA

NOTES

Abbreviations: p.=page; śl.=śloka or stanza; l.=line.

Mitralâbha: mitra, a friend, and lâbha, gaining.

p. 3, śl. 1. 'Siva, the deity invoked at the beginning of the *Hitopadesa*, is often represented as wearing the crescent moon (or the new moon) for his crest. 'Siva does not appear by name at a very early period in the Hindû mythology, but in the Vedas the same deity is very frequently invoked as Rudra. Rudra means the "Roarer" or "Howler": he is the god of the storms and the father of the Maruts, who are represented as storm deities, armed with lightning and thunderbolts. In after-times he was developed into the deity 'Siva, which means the kindly, beneficent, propitious. In the Vedas he is sometimes represented as the destroying influence, sometimes as the restorer.

The 'Siva of the Hindû, developed in the course of ages from the Rudra of the Vedas, is the third person of the Hindû triad. As Mahâkâla (the great black deity) he is the destroying influence. But destruction implies restoration, and therefore he is 'Siva the kindly, the auspicious, and under that aspect is Mahâdeva the great god, or Îsvara the supreme lord. As the restorer and reproducer he is worshipped under his symbol the lingam, along with the representation of his 'Saktî or female energy called Devî.

He also appears in a third character as the great

ascetic (Mahâyogî)—the ideal and personification of penance and meditation, by means of which he has gained unlimited spiritual influence. The legends and powers ascribed to him are almost endless, and under one form or another he has gained widespread veneration and worship.

p. 3, śl. 2. The word Hitopadeśa is a compound made up of "hita," a past participle meaning salutary, and "upadeśa," counsel. By the rules of combination the "a" of the preceding word followed by the "u" of that joined on to it coalesces into "o"; hence "hita"+"upadeśa" becomes hitopadeśa.

p. 4, l. 11. Pâtaliputra is the Palibothra of the Greek writers. Arrian, in his *Indikê*, says that "the largest city among the Indians is called Palibothra, and that it is in the land of the Prasiai, where the river Erannoboa runs into the Ganges. The Prasiai were a large and powerful tribe living on the Ganges, who in the time of Seleucus I were governed by Chandragupta, whom we have in Arrian under the Greek form "Sandracottos."

Pâtaliputra is identified with the modern Patna.

p. 4, l. 12. Bhâgîrathî is another name for the Ganges, derived from Bhagîratha, a Hindû saint who by means of his austerities and penances was said to have persuaded 'Siva to allow the Ganges to descend from heaven to earth.

p. 4, l. 13. Sudarśana means "good looking."

p. 5, śl. 15. This śloka is a little difficult to translate and a little difficult to explain. The translation in the text would perhaps be clearer if it ran: "If a woman be a mother to him at whose name, etc." Mr. F. W. Thomas, the librarian at the India Office, has kindly suggested the following: "If in a man, for whom at the very commencement of counting the host of meritorious people, the chalk does not fall with haste, his mother can be said to be possessed of a son—say, what is a barren woman like?"

The chalk must be put to the writing tablet to mark the excellencies of the person whose name is mentioned, at once, without any doubt or hesitation. The woman, therefore, who has a son about whose good qualities there is some doubt, and whose virtues are not apparent, may as well have none.

p. 6, śl. 28. Nîlakaṇṭha, the "blue-throated one," a name of 'Siva, so called because his neck became blue after drinking up the deadly poison which would otherwise have destroyed the world. The reference to him here is in the character of the naked ascetic, Digambara, one who "has the sky for his garment."

Hari, another name for Vishṇu, is represented as asleep on the serpent 'Sesha, and moving over the waters which covered the world before the Creation. This idea rather suggests Genesis I. 2.

p. 7, śl. 30. The Sesamum plant, the Hindû name for which is "tila," bears an oily seed, and is much used in Indian cookery.

p. 8, l. 16. "The Sacred Scriptures." 'Sâstra, which I have translated thus, means any religious or scientific treatise, or any religious book of divine authority; the expression 'Sâstra may even be applied to the Veda.

p. 8, l. 18. "Political and social science," nîti-śâstra, i.e. the "śâstras" which treat of "nîti." Nîti, among other things, such as moral conduct, policy, etc., means "political economy, statesmanship."

p. 8, l. 27. Vishnuśarman, i.e. whose refuge is Vishṇu. 'Sarman is the ordinary affix to the names of Brâhmans.

p. 8, l. 29. Vrihaspati is regarded as the deity who presides over speech.

p. 10, l. 15. The 'Sâlmali is the Seemul, or silk cotton tree (*Bombax heptaphyllum*).

p. 10, l. 20. Laghupatanaka = quickly flying.

p. 11, l. 10. Chitragrîva = speckled neck.

p. 12, l. 8. Amrit, the nectar which confers immortality on the drinker.

p. 13. śl, 10. This śloka is a quotation from the Mahâbhârata. Pâṇḍu was the brother of Dhritarâshtra. He had five sons, the five Pâṇḍavas, who are the heroes of the great Hindû epic, the Mahâbhârata.

p. 17, śl. 30. We are told that in India when the cow is milked the calf is tied to her with a rope, otherwise she will not allow the milk to flow.

p. 18, l. 21. Hiranyaka = the golden.

p. 18, l. 23. Gandakî, a river in Oude.

p. 21, l. 16. Yojana = about 9 English miles.

p. 22, l. 31. Magadhadésa, the country of South Behar.

p. 23, l. 8. Kshudrabuddhi = slow-witted.

p. 23, l. 17. Subuddhi = wise.

p. 24, l. 2. Gridhrakuta = vulture peak.

p. 24, l. 11. Dîrghakarṇa = long ears.

p. 25, l. 10. The Chândrâyana penance consists in diminishing the daily consumption of food during one half of the moon's course, until the quantity is reduced to 0, and then increasing it again for the fortnight of the moon's increase.

p. 26, śl. 63. "A man of the lowest class"; in orig. a Chânḍâla, the name of a very low and degraded tribe.

p. 29, l. 12. Sunday, bhaṭṭâraka vâra, the day of the great lord, i.e. of the Sun.

p. 35, l. 11. Dandaka, a forest of vast size, lying between the Godâvarî and the Narmadâ. This forest is the scene of many of the adventures of Râma and Sîtâ.

p. 35, l. 12. Karpûragama = the (lake) yellowish white, as camphor.

p. 35, l. 14. Manthara = slow.

p. 38, l. 6. Gaur or Gauḍa is a province in the central part of Bengal.

p. 46, śl. 162. Keśava = having long and beautiful hair; a name of Vishṇu or Krishṇa.

p. 48, l. 5. Bhairava = the terrible.

p. 48, l. 6. Kalyânakaṭaka = the happy town.

p. 48, l. 7. The Vindhya forest consists of the mountains which stretch across India and divide the Madhya-deśa, or "middle land," namely Hindûstan, from the Deccan.

p. 48, l. 24. Dîrgharâva = long yell.

p. 52, l. 32. Chitrânga = dappled body.

p. 54, l. 13. Kalinga is a district on the western coast of India, extending from a little below Kaṭaka (Cuttack), in Bengal, to Madras.

p. 54, l. 17. Chandrabhâgâ = the Chenab, one of the five streams of the Panjâb.

p. 55. l. 11. Kanyakubjâ, or Kanyâkubja. The modern name of this city is Kanauj. In ancient times this city was situated on the Kâlînadî, a tributary of the Ganges, in the district now called Furuckabad. The name of the town signifies "the crooked damsel," and has reference to a legend relating how the hundred daughters of King Kuśanâbha were all made crooked by Vâyu for refusing to comply with his advances. The ruins of the ancient city are said to occupy an area of many miles.

p. 61, śl. 223. Mitram = a friend.

p. 65. Suhridbheda. Suhrid = having a kind heart, a friend; bheda, breaking.

p. 65, l. 14. Dakshinapatha, the southern portion of the peninsula of India, now called the Deccan.

p. 65, l. 16. Vardhamâna = the prospering, thriving.

p. 67, l. 12. Kashmîr, a district north of the Panjâb.

p. 67, l. 20. Durga = hard to pass.

p. 68, l. 18. Pingalaka = tawny.

p. 68, l. 27. The Jumna (anciently Yamunâ) is a river in the N. W. Provinces.

p. 70, śl. 27. Chowries (châmara in the Sk.). The tail of a kind of ox which is used to keep the flies off, and is one of the symbols of royalty. This śloka suggests the stories of Joseph, Haman, etc., in the Old Testament.

p. 72, l. 1. Vârâṇasî. The sacred city of Benares.

p. 78, śl. 61. Vrihaspati. *v.* note on Mitralâbha, p. 8, l. 29.

p. 84, l. 6. Arbuda 'Sikhara, a mountain in the west of India, generally called Abû. It was a noted place of pilgrimage to which the Tains used to resort.

p. 84, l. 7. Mahâvikrama = a mighty force.

p. 86, śl. 85. The story referred to is as follows: 'Siśupâla was a king of Cheḍi who opposed the worship of Krishṇa, and at a great sacrifice in honour of this deity, who was present himself in person, reviled him as a contemptible being, and challenged him to fight. Krishṇa thereupon immediately struck off 'Siśupâla's head with the sharp discus or quoit which he carried.

p. 87, l. 1. Brahmapura and 'Srîparvata are probably imaginary places.

p. 87, l. 4. Ghantâkarṇa = one who has ears decorated with bells.

p. 88, l. 8. Stabdhakarna = one with stiff ears.

p. 92, l. 14. Svarnarekhâ = the streak of gold.

p. 92, l. 21. Kânchanapura = golden town.

p. 92, l. 22. Vîravikrama = mighty in valour.

p. 92, l. 25. Kandarpaketu = the ensign of Kâma (the Hindû Cupid).

p. 93, l. 5. Jîmûtaketu = the ensign of the Sun.

p. 93, l. 6. Singhaladvîpa = the island of Ceylon.

p. 93, l. 13. Lakshmî or 'Srî, the goddess of Fortune, wife of Vishṇu, mother of Kâma (the Hindû Cupid). According to one legend she sprang like Aphrodité from the foam of the ocean, bearing a lotus in her hand. But there are various legends relating to her origin and existence.

p. 93, l. 26. Ratnamanjarî may mean "a row of jewels" or "jewelled bud."

p. 93, l. 26. Kandarpakelî = the spirit of Kandarpa or Kâma (*see* above, l. 13).

p. 93, l. 27. Vidyâdharas = "possessors of knowledge." The Vidyâdharas are a class of inferior deities inhabiting the regions between the earth and the sky. They are represented as having kings and chiefs of their own, but have much intercourse with men and intermarry with them. The hero and many of the characters of the "Nâgânanda," a Buddhist drama, are represented as Vidyâdharas. Cf. Gen. VI. 2, for the same idea.

p. 95, l. 17. Yama in the Hindû mythology is the equivalent of the Greek Minos. He is represented as judging the dead in the after-world, and rewarding them according to their deserts.

p. 95, l. 29. The Malaya mountains are the hills of Malabar, the southern part of the Western Ghâts.

p. 97, l. 5. Dvârâvatî = "the city of many gates." Krishna's capital in Gujarat, also called Abdhi nagarî = "the city of ocean." The town is now called Dwarka; it was supposed to have been submerged by the ocean.

p. 99, l. 9. In Story IX, which follows, the Rabbit is represented in the character with which he is invested in the famous "Songs and Sayings of Uncle Remus."

p. 106, l. 25. Garuḍa, a mythical bird of enormous size, on which Vishnu rides. He is the king of birds, and is represented as having the head, wings, and claws of an eagle, and the body and limbs of a man. Garuḍa has a very important part in the drama referred to above (note on p. 93, l. 27), where he devours a Nâga, or serpent, daily, and is bought off by Jîmûtavâhana, the king of the Nâgas, who by the sacrifice of himself to Garuḍa, converts the bird king and saves his people.

p. 106, l. 28. Nârâyana, a patronymical form from "Nara," the original man, the spirit which pervades the universe. Nârâyana, therefore, is the "Son of the original pervading spirit." Other theories explanatory of the name are to be found in the elaborate Hindû mythology, but perhaps it may be sufficient to say that in later times the appellation was generally given to Vishnu.

p. 117. Vigraha = stretching things apart from one another; hence division, quarrels, war.

p. 117, l. 15. Padmakelî = the sport of the lotuses.

p. 117, l. 15. Karpûradvîpa = camphor island.

p. 117, l. 17. Hiraṇyagarbha = filled with (or made of) gold.

p. 118, l. 10. Dîrghamukha = long bill.

p. 118, l. 17. Jambudvîpa, one of the seven divisions which make up the world according to the Hindû fable.

p. 118, l. 18. Chitravarṇa = of many (or variegated) colours.

p. 119, l. 13. The Narmadâ (now commonly called the Nerbudda) rises in the Vindhya hills and flows into the Gulf of Cambay. This river was looked on with special veneration as being sacred, and was personified.

p. 120, l. 25. Hastinâpura, the capital city of the Kauravas, for which the great war was waged, described in the Mahâbhârata. It was situated about fifty miles north-east of the modern Delhi, on the banks of an old channel of the Ganges, and was said to have been founded by a king bearing the name of Hastin. The ruins are still traceable. Hastin also means "an elephant," and the name is otherwise explained as "Elephant city."

p. 122, l. 7. For the craft displayed by the

Rabbits in this story compare Story IX, Suhrid-bheda (p. 99, l. 9).

p. 124, l. 21. Chakravâka. This bird is the "ruddy goose," or Brâhmany duck.

p. 124, l. 22. Sarvajna = all knowing.

p. 125, l. 32. For the black poison staining 'Siva's neck see note on p. 6, śl. 28.

p. 126, l. 20. Ujjayinî = the modern Ujjein, a city of Central India. It was known to the Greeks as Ozênê. It was the capital of Vikramâditya, who was supposed to have reigned about 57 B.C. Ujjayinî was one of the seven sacred cities.

p. 127, l. 22. For Garuḍa see note on p. 106, l. 25.

p. 128, l. 19. Mandamati = slow-witted, stupid.

p. 128, l. 20. 'Srînagara = the city of Fortune. There are two towns bearing this name.

p. 135, l. 18. Sârasa = the Indian crane.

p. 136, l. 6. Meghavarṇa = cloud colour, i.e. black as a cloud.

p. 138, śl. 59. Chanakya was a celebrated Brâhman, who took a leading part in the destruction of a dynasty called the Nandas. He was a great master of diplomacy and artifice, and is said to be the author of a work on policy.

p. 140, l. 16. Dûradarśîn = the far-seeing.

p. 142, l. 1. Kshâtriya, the second of the four castes or varṇas, whose duty it is to rule and fight. The four castes are as follows :—

1. Brâhman, sacerdotal and learned.
2. Kshâtriya, regal and warrior.
3. Vaiśya, agricultural and trading.
4. 'Sûdra, the servile caste, whose duty it is to serve the first three.

The first three castes were called dvi-ja, "twice-born," because they were invested with the sacred thread whereby they were "regenerated" or born again. It is said that at the present time there are no pure Kshâtriyas existing, the Brâhman caste being the only one that remains pure and unmixed.

p. 142, l. 11. Vâchaspati = the lord of speech; in the Hindû mythology the preceptor of the gods. There was also a grammarian and writer of this name.

p. 142, l. 23. For the Malaya mountain see note on p. 95, l. 29.

p. 143, l. 14. 'Sûdraka was a king of a country and people in South India called Andhra. The dynasty to which he belonged flourished about the beginning of the Christian Era.

p. 143, l. 20. Karpûramanjarî = camphor-stalk.

p. 143, l. 23. Râjaputra, the son of a king, a member of the Kshâtriya caste. The Râjputs claim to be descended from the Kshâtriyas.

p. 145, l. 12. "I am the Fortune of King 'Sûdraka." The word for Fortune is "Lakshmî," used here in personified form.

p. 145, l. 19. 'Saktidhara = a spearman.

p. 145, l. 20. Durgâ = the inaccessible, known otherwise as Devî, "the goddess." She is the wife of 'Siva in the Hindû mythology, and has various attributes. She is generally worshipped and propitiated as a fierce and savage deity, delighting in bloodshed and in all kinds of disgusting and indecent orgies.

p. 145, l. 23. Lakshmî (*see* above, p. 145, l. 12).

p. 147, l. 16. Karnâṭa, a district in the central district of the peninsula of India. From this word comes the name "Carnatic."

p. 148, l. 5. Ayodhyâ was the capital of Ikshwâku, the reputed founder of the Sola dynasty. Max Müller takes Ikshwâku not as the name of a king but of a people. The modern name of Ayodhyâ is Oude, but the exact site of the ancient town has not been ascertained.

p. 161. Sandhi = combination, union.

p. 162, l. 17. Magadhadeśa (*see* note on p. 22, l. 31).

p. 162, l. 17. Phullotpala = phulla + utpala, flowering lotus.

p. 162, l. 20. Kambugrîva = shell neck.

p. 163, l. 3. Anâgatavidhâtâ = one who arranges for events not yet come, provident.

p. 163, l. 3. Pratyutpannamati = having a mind ready in present emergencies.

p. 163, l. 4. Yadbhavishyat = one who believes in the overruling power of fate.

p. 163, l. 25. Vikramapura, name of a town, perhaps imaginary.

p. 163, l. 26. Ratnaprabhâ = having the splendour of jewels.

p. 165, l. 25. Gridmakûṭa = peak of the Vulture.

p. 165, l. 26. Revâ, a name for the River Narmadâ (*see* note on p. 119, l. 13).

p. 168, l. 27. Gautama is a name of patronymical form applied to a variety of deities and men. The forest of Gautama is probably an imaginary title.

p. 170, l. 8. Malva = thoughtless, foolish. Perhaps a name invented for an imaginary country, referring to the foolishness of the fish who confided in their natural enemy, the Crane.

p. 170, l. 9. Padmagarbha = lotus bearing.

p. 172, l. 18. Devîkoṭṭa = the castle of the goddess Devî or Durgâ.

p. 172, l. 18. Devaśarman = whose refuge is the deity.

p. 174, l. 15. For Vrihaspatî *see* note on Mitralâbha, p. 8, l. 29.

p. 174, l. 20. Sunda and Upasunda were two Daityas or demigods.

p. 174, l. 26. "The deity whose crest is the half-moon" (or new moon) (*see* note on p. 1, śl. 1).

p. 175, l. 8. Parvatî is another name for Devî or Durgâ (*see* note on p. 145, l. 20).

p. 175, śl. 25. For the four castes see note on

p. 142, l. 1. The advice given by 'Siva in the form of a Brâhman to Sunda and Upasunda corresponds with that given by Krishṇa in the Bhagavadgîtâ to Arjuna, the hero of the Pândavas.

When Arjuna, with Krishṇa for his charioteer, was facing his cousins the Kauravas, in the great fight for the recovery of the kingdom out of which the Pândavas had been cheated by a Kaurava prince, he became filled with compassion and hesitated to make the attack. Krishṇa addresses him :—

"Considering thine own duty as a Kshâtriya thou art not right to waver. For there is nothing better for a Kshâtriya than lawful war. Happy are the warriors who undertake such a war spontaneously offered to them—an open door to heaven. But if thou wilt not join in this lawful fight, thou abandonest thine own duty and glory, and contractest a crime. . . . Therefore arise! make up thy mind to fight" (Bhagavadgîtâ, chap. II.).

p. 180, l. 15 Gauḍa, also Gaura, the ancient name for Central Bengal and of the capital of the country of the same name. The remains of the town are still in existence.

p. 180, l. 15. Yajnaśarma = whose refuge is sacrifice.

p. 181, l. 16. Madotkaṭa = mada-utkaṭa, excited by passion.

p. 181, l. 23. Chitrakarṇa = "strange-ear," or perhaps rough-eared.

p. 184, l. 28. Mandavisarpa = slow crawler.

p. 185, l. 14. Suśîla = having an amiable disposition.

p. 187, l. 11. Sagara, a king of Ayodhyâ (the modern Oude), the hero of many exploits. He is said to have subdued a vast number of tribes, among them one called the "Yavanas," who are identified with the Greeks, or "Ionians." We come across the same people in the Old Testament under the name of "Javan" (Gen. X. 2; I Chron. I. 5; Isa. LXVI. 19; Ezek. XXVII. 13, 19). Pâṇini the grammarian speaks of the writings of the Yavanas. These Yavanas may be identified with the Macedonian Greeks who settled on the N.W. frontier. Sagara entirely subdued them, and "made them shave their heads entirely." The interest of these Yavanas is contained in the fact that they constitute the connecting link between India and Europe, and are a valuable asset in the calculation of Indian dates and the construction of Indian history.

p. 191, l. 6. Ujjayinî (*see* note on p. 126, l. 20.)

p. 191, l. 13. Pârvanaśrâddha, a sacrifice offered at the "parvan," a special period of the year, such as the equinox, or the conjunction of the sun and moon. The Pârvanaśrâddha consisted in solemn funeral offerings to the Manes of ancestors. In this sacrifice double oblations were offered to the father, grandfather, and great-grandfather on both sides, and the crumbs from these oblations to the remoter ancestors. Making this offering was part of the privileges of the Sacred Caste.

p. 195, l. 18. Dûradarśîn, the Vulture, who is represented as a learned, farseeing person, enumerates sixteen different kinds of alliances on which peace may be formed. To go through all the sixteen would be tedious and unedifying, and I have therefore considerably abbreviated the Vulture's advice. The peace which Dûradarśîn calls the "Golden" he explains as the alliance made between good men, based upon friendship, called "Sangata" (union through friendship). The duration is for life; its object is identity of purpose; and it is not broken either by prosperity or adversity. From its transcendent excellence it is like gold, and for this reason it is called by those skilled in diplomacy the Golden.

W. Brendon and Son, Limited, Plymouth.

Published by

Facsimile Publisher
Ashok Vihar, Delhi-110052 (India)
Website: www.facsimilepublisher.com

Distributed by

Gyan Books Pvt. Ltd.
5, Ansari Road, Daryaganj, New Delhi-110002 (India)
E-mail: books@gyanbooks.com, Website: www.gyanbooks.com

2 222000 000585